SECRET OF MATURITY

FOURTH EDITION

Kevin Everett FitzMaurice, M.S.

Begin

Title

Secret of Maturity

FitzMaurice Publishers

kevinfitzmaurice.com

Subtitle

Fourth Edition

FitzMaurice Publishers

kevinfitzmaurice.com

Copyright

FitzMaurice, Kevin Everett.

Secret of Maturity: Fourth Edition.

1. Self-help. 2. Psychology. 3. Philosophy.

ISBN

ISBN 978-1-521819-692

FitzMaurice Publishers, Portland, Oregon

kevinfitzmaurice.com

Dedication

This book is dedicated to all those who want to know what it means to live an emotionally mature life despite living in an increasingly emotionally immature world.

Description

This book describes maturity in understandable and practical terms. If you want to know what it means to be mature, this book is for you. If you want to know how to live a mature life, this book is for you. If you want to grow up or know what it means to grow up, this book is for you.

With all our means of communication and education, how is it possible that many fundamental concepts and principles continue to remain a secret or a mystery to most people? What kind of educational system can call itself "education" and fail to discuss and explore fundamental human qualities like maturity?

The research for this book uncovered a myriad of ways of approaching the same basic answer for the secret of maturity: maturity is responsibility. Most of the answers to "What is maturity?" come from either psychology or philosophy. The answers are listed or briefly described throughout the text, but it is your job to decide what to do with all the answers. So be responsible for how you assimilate the answers and put them into practice.

Quite a few of the paragraphs in this book summarize concepts that are expounded in entire volumes elsewhere. Since this book is so condensed, it will be most effective after it has been read and studied many times.

Might we suggest that you first pursue those concepts that strike you as personally relevant? That will do you the most good today, because those concepts will be emotionally valuable to you. Read the suggested references to those concepts, and locate other related works at the library or through Internet searches.

If you learn and apply the lessons contained in this book, results are guaranteed. Anyone who learns to live maturely will find that he or she is in better health, because he or she can handle stress better. Anyone who learns to live maturely will find that he or she has a better love life, because he or she can handle interpersonal relationships and communication better. Anyone who learns to live maturely will find that he or she has a better career or work experience, because he or she can better handle challenges, conflicts, stressors, work politics, and work pressures.

> Finally, brethren, whatsoever things are true, whatsoever things are honest, whatsoever things are just, whatsoever things are pure, whatsoever things are lovely, whatsoever things are of good report; if there be any virtue, and if there be any praise, think on these things.
>
> —Philippians 4:8

10 Approaches to Sanity

FitzMaurice's ebooks offer different approaches for you to choose to improve your physical, mental, emotional, and relational well-being. Here are ten of them.

1. In *Ego*, discover proven methods that you can use to reduce your devotion to and dependence upon ego. The less ego you have, the more passionate and productive your life will be. Reducing ego also allows you to be free, happy, spontaneous, compassionate, and more creative. Choose to be your real self.

2. In *Garden*, discover Cognitive Behavioral Therapy (CBT) methods for sorting out which thoughts work for you and which thoughts work against you. Also learn how to increase your productive thoughts and decrease your unproductive thoughts, in order to improve your coping, problem-solving, relationships, health, and happiness. Choose your feelings.

3. In *Breathe*, discover methods for congruence, relief, self-relaxation, self-calming, and self-centering. With practice, the methods' positive effects come almost instantaneously. You can lower your stress and improve your physical, relational, mental, and emotional health and happiness now. Choose tranquility.

4. In *Attitude Is All You Need! Second Edition*, discover methods to sort out which attitudes are working for you and which attitudes are working against you. Also learn how to increase your productive attitudes and to decrease your unproductive attitudes, in order to free yourself from the negative influence of detrimental attitudes and to improve your health and happiness. Choose your attitude.

5. In Not, discover how to save yourself from the number one mistake that underlies failure and error. Learn how to be a more effective parent, coach, and leader by learning to encourage, inspire, and motivate others more powerfully. Stop doing the opposite of what you want to do. Also learn how to choose to live a positive life over the negative "not" trap. Choose success.

6. In Garbage Rules, be confronted with your reliance on mental garbage and the resulting garbage that reliance brings into your life. Be paradoxically motivated to switch to healthier and happier thinking and feeling styles by facing the absurdity of focusing on garbage. This is a program of well-being for beginners, those in early recovery, and people in 12-step groups. Choose change.

7. In the three books Something For Nothing, Anything Goes, and Acid Test, and the seven released books in the 3D: Daily Dose of Discernment series, find sayings and aphorisms on many topics that you can use for introspection, contemplation, meditation, and mental exercise. Choose intelligence.

8. In *Planet Earth: Insane Asylum, Second Edition*, discover how human conditioning systems are insane on many levels and for many reasons. Yes, human educational systems, political systems, and social systems are designed to keep you insane. Yes, human belief systems and preferred thinking styles are insane. Need examples or proof? This book is for you.

9. In *Stress for Success, Second Edition*, discover how stress is misunderstood and misused. Learn how stress is your best friend. Improve how and when you cope and problem-solve and how often you cope and problem-solve. Increase how often you achieve and contribute by taking charge of your stress. Choose good stress, not bad stress.

10. In *Games Ego Plays*, discover the psychological or ego games that people play with each other, both in private and in their social relationships. Wouldn't it be great to be able to get out of ego games without conflict, when others intend to play them at your expense? Wouldn't it be great to recognize an ego game from the start, so that you might either redirect the interaction in a healthy way or avoid being locked into a stressful and unproductive ego game? Wouldn't it be great to relate with others in ways that don't involve ego games, even though we are all conditioned and trained to play psychological games? Learn how with this book. Choose to be game free.

Experiment with the ebooks until you discover the approach or two that works best for you. Worry not if your choices are the best for anyone else.

> Today you can do the good more and the bad less.
>
> —Kevin Everett FitzMaurice

C1: What Is Maturity?

Happiness does not depend on outward things, but on the way we see them.

—Leo Tolstoy

Maturity Defined

Responsibility is the price of greatness.

—Winston S. Churchill

Responsibility is the great developer.

—Louis D. Brandeis

Responsibility is a detachable burden easily shifted to the shoulder of God, Fate, Fortune, Luck, or one's neighbor.

—Ambrose Bierce, *The Devil's Dictionary*

Maturity is responsibility. Maturity is holding yourself responsible before you hold anyone or anything else responsible. Maturity is looking to find the fault within yourself before looking at people, places, or things for the cause of the problem. Maturity is the act of taking personal responsibility for all aspects of your life. Maturity is the response of the integrated individual to challenging times and circumstances.

Maturity is demonstrated by rational responses to irrational events. Maturity is demonstrated by showing equanimity in the face of certain adversity. Maturity is demonstrated by the acceptance of all things as they are.

The highest maturity comes when you look for your inner choices that have determined your outer fate. For example, when you make a mistake or have an accident, you do not blame even chance, let alone others. Instead, you examine your intentions, feelings, and thoughts to see how you chose to serve that outcome. This level of maturity requires a degree of internal awareness that is as uncommon as it is wise.

> A man of genius makes no mistakes. His errors are volitional and are the portals of discovery.
>
> —James Joyce

Maturity's Source: Emotional Responsibility

> If you are distressed by anything external, the pain is not due to the thing itself but to your own estimate of it: and this you have power to revoke at any moment.
>
> —Marcus Aurelius

The ultimate secret of maturity is that maturity is entirely dependent upon *emotional responsibility.* Emotional responsibility is the realization and practice of the principle that you alone can and do decide how you will feel. Without emotional responsibility, you will react immaturely to your unpleasant feelings, with whining, blaming, and damning. Since the emotionally immature person believes events, others, and life cause his or her feelings, then he or she must try to control or change events, others, and life to control how he or she feels. Since people fail to control events, others, and life, they become frustrated, hurt, and angry. They then react irrationally, demandingly, and immaturely to events, others, and life.

> If people can't control their own emotions, then they have to start trying to control other people's behavior.

–Robin Skynner

Many misguided people believe that they can cause feelings in others but not in themselves. Many unthinking counselors and therapists want their clients to be responsible for causing feelings in spouses and family members, but not for causing feelings in themselves. This expectation is quite backwards, if you think about it scientifically. You are responsible for your thoughts, feelings, and actions, but you are not responsible for the thoughts, feelings, or actions of others.

Yes, you are responsible for *influencing* the thoughts, feelings, and actions of others; however, you can only be held responsible for causing the thoughts, feelings, and actions of other people under special circumstances. For instance, if you are in charge of a concentration camp, then you have enough power, control, and means to control people in many ways. Still, neurologist and psychiatrist Victor Frankl in his world-famous book, *Man's Search for Meaning,* uses his experiences in concentration camps to prove that humans are always free to choose in the most important ways.

Below are seven reasons for why you alone are responsible for how you feel. More reasons could be given, but the following seven should suffice to prove the point of emotional responsibility.

7 Reasons for Emotional Responsibility

There are more than seven reasons for the fact that people are responsible for their emotions. However, the seven reasons listed here imply, include, and suggest other reasons while providing a concise list for your consideration. In *C8: Assorted Additions* you can also find “Table: 12 Reasons Emotionally Responsible”.

1. You decide what to identify as self (think “this is me”) and what to keep your identity detached from. Whatever you identify with as self will cause you to have feelings. And each time you identity with something, it will cause you to have new or more feelings about that something.

> Keeping something out of your identity keeps its intensity low: detached. Eating, owning, or taking something into your identity dramatically increases the intensity of its experience for you: attached.

2. You decide what to experience with your heart, and what to stay emotionally detached from with your heart. Whatever you experience with your heart will cause you to have feelings. And whatever you keep re-experiencing with your heart will cause you to have new or more feelings about that thing you are re-experiencing.

Keeping something out of your heart keeps that something's intensity low. Eating, owning, or taking something into your heart dramatically increases the intensity of that something for you.

3. You decide what to pay attention to, what to remember, and what to think about—or what to let naturally pass through your mind. Whatever you dwell on, loop on, or repeat over and over in your mind will affect you emotionally. And the more you obsess about something, the more that thing will affect you because of its greater frequency, intensity, and duration in your mind and thoughts.

4. You decide what to try to control or change and what to accept as-is. Whatever you try to control or change will affect you emotionally. And the harder you try to control or change something, the more that thing will affect you because of its greater frequency, intensity, and duration in your thoughts and feelings.

5. You decide what to consider or construe as important or unimportant. Whatever you view as important will affect you emotionally. And the more importance you place on something, the greater that thing will affect you because of its greater frequency, intensity, and duration inside of you.

6. You are responsible for your heart, soul, mind, identity, attention, awareness, and memory. Any of these can affect you emotionally more than either your body or your environment can affect you emotionally, for the reasons given in number seven below.

7. Science teaches us that it is the proximity, frequency, intensity, and duration of signals that determines the impact or the force of signals experienced. Your mind can cause signals that are closer to you, that are more frequent, that are stronger, and that endure longer than any signals that either your body or your environment can cause. Hence, the signals in your mind can and do affect you more than either your bodily or your environmental signals can or do affect you.

> Signals are anything that you receive from the result of sensing, of using your senses. For example, anything you notice that you are hearing, such as a loud noise or another person talking, can be understood as a signal for or to your sense of hearing.

Maturity comes from emotional maturity, and emotional maturity comes from emotional responsibility. Emotional responsibility comes from learning to be aware of how you cause your feelings, and from learning the emotional skills that allow you to release and free yourself of any unwanted feeling.

To maintain your belief in emotional responsibility, you need to stand against the social and common beliefs in your having magically induced emotions, emotions caused by the voodoo dolls in the minds of others, and emotions caused by the extrasensory perception abilities (ESP) of others. (For more on the nature of emotions, read FitzMaurice's ebooks *Attitude Is All You Need, Second Edition* and *Garden*.)

Table: Summary of 7 Reasons

7 Reasons: Emotional Responsibility	
1	I decide what to identify with or not.
2	I decide what to take to heart or not.
3	I decide what to remember and think about.
4	I decide what to try to change or to control.
5	I decide what to consider important or not.
6	I am responsible for my heart, soul, and mind.
7	I'm responsible for the strength of my signals.
More information: *Secret of Maturity, Fourth Edition*	
Copyright © 2017 by Kevin Everett FitzMaurice	https://kevinfitzmaurice.com

Emotional Responsibility Used & Abused

> Many modern psychotherapists have adopted as their credo, Socrates' declaration that "the unexamined life is not worth living." We should pledge ourselves to the proposition that the irresponsible life is not worth living.
>
> —Thomas S. Szasz

You need to be responsible toward—but not for—people. This need puts your burden of responsibility on your behavior toward people, not for the other person's behavior or responses.

Unfortunately, the concept of emotional responsibility is abused by some to excuse their actions and to avoid taking responsibility for the impacts of their actions. It is true that you are never responsible for the feelings of others, but it is also true that you are always responsible for what you send out, communicate, or do that can affect others.

Learning that you are responsible—for both what you take inside, and how you interpret and make use of what you take inside—does not mean that you are no longer responsible for what you send out to be taken inside by others. You can be a stimulus that elicits either good or bad:

you choose all the signals that you send out—haptic (contact or touch), body expressions or language, and verbal (sounds and words) signals.

Yes, it is true that others are free to respond to what you send out, according to their own choices—regardless of what you send out to hook them, tempt them, pressure them, or to cause a predictable response in them. But does that mean you should intentionally make it challenging or difficult for people to respond peacefully? No, it does not if compassion and peaceful relations are your goals. Yes, you can try to annoy or hurt others to feel power and pride, but there are better options for the mature.

Blame Game

The real problem with emotional responsibility is that it ends our favorite emotional game: the *Blame Game*. We play the Blame Game by hating, persecuting, or blaming others for our feelings, while also reacting to our feelings with a helpless, hopeless, or victim attitude. (Optionally, we can play the Blame Game with our conscience, our body, places, things, events, or even God.)

Emotional responsibility ends the Blame Game because it portrays us as responsible: We have control over all our responses, both inside and outside of our bodies, that result in our feelings.

In the past, our only solution or temporary escape from the Blame Game was to play or to find someone (dependency) or something (addiction) else to play the buffer game for us—to play fixer, helper, or rescuer for our or others' feelings. Transactional Analysis (TA) has a diagram for the structure of this buffer game, called the Karpman Drama Triangle. (For more information, see *Born to Win: Transactional Analysis with Gestalt Experiments* by Muriel James and Dorothy Jongeward.)

Lawmakers, judges, social workers, and therapists often fall into the "rescuer" position of the drama triangle. This position is taken because these professionals have not dealt with their own codependency issues, else they lack a systems perspective and tend to think in fragmentary ways. In any event, such professionals unthinkingly continue to see and treat one person as the victim and another person as the persecutor. Such linear thinking is naïve at best, and at worst it continues the cycle of the drama triangle by socializing the roles and continuing the triangle with new players.

Perhaps if professionals were educated about the drama triangle system and the interdependence of its roles, then they could learn to become more constructive and socially responsible to break the drama-triangle cycle. The current efforts of many professions only support, determine, and enable the very behaviors those professions object to. For instance, social workers tend to institutionalize, feed, and multiply any social game they enter. As another example, it is well-known that prisons are college for criminals and not rehabilitation for criminals.

For in-depth analysis and understand of human games on both intrapersonal and interpersonal levels, read Games Ego Plays. In this book, human games are diagramed and explained from the perspective of ego rewards and punishments.

The Secret of Maturity

> We who lived in concentration camps can remember the men who walked through the huts comforting others, giving away their last piece[s] of bread. They offer sufficient proof that everything can be taken from a man but one thing: the last of the human freedoms—to choose one's attitude in any given set of circumstances, to choose one's own way.
>
> —Victor E. Frankl

The secret of maturity is that it does not come with age but from taking 100% responsibility for your thoughts, feelings, actions, and experiences, and by taking 0% responsibility for the thoughts, feelings, actions, and experiences of others.

The degree of your maturity equals the degree of your responsibility for your life.

Please remember that your personal responsibility also includes your intentions for how you will affect others. While others determine how what you say affects them, you can intend to hurt others with meanness or sarcasm. Or, you can intend to inspire and uplift others with hope and insights. Others' misunderstandings of your intentions are not your responsibility, but for the sake of improved results when communicating with others, the wise learn to adapt, adjust, and accommodate their speech for their audience.

Observable characteristics of the mature person includes their having:

• An inner dialogue punctuated by silence instead of self-talk.

• Both individual and social concerns.

• Integration between his or her intentions and actions.

• Integration between his or her thoughts and feelings.

• More activities that he or she participates in than activities wherein he or she is only an observer.

• The ability to admit his or her actions are both selfish and unselfish.

• The ability to choose rather than react under most circumstances.

• ~~The ability to suffer short-term discomfort for long-term rewards~~.

• The habit of continually testing everything.

• The habit of testing and disputing his or her self-talk.

• The tendency to be proactive rather than reactive.

Truly mature people are so detached from others that they can love their enemies, bless those who curse them, do good to those who hate them, and pray for those who despitefully use and persecute them. (See Matthew 5:44.)

Table: 5 Questions on Responsibility

Below is a table containing five simple questions to use to test if you are emotionally responsible or mature, or not. "Integrity" is used in the table in the sense of holding together, of holding fast to one's primary purpose, of soundness, and of wholeness. Consider this example usage: "The ship's integrity was lost when she ran aground on treacherous costal rocks causing her to sink with the incoming tide."

5 Questions: Emotional Responsibility	
1	Can you perceive, think, feel, or experience differently from the groups you belong to?
2	Can you easily laugh at yourself and your failings?
3	Do you have enough integrity that pressures from circumstances or groups cannot break your beliefs, ideals, or morals?
4	Do your hardships, trials, tribulations, or sufferings ennoble or weaken you?
5	Do your hardships, trials, tribulations, or sufferings bring out your highest or lowest attitudes and responses?
More information: *Secret of Maturity, Fourth Edition*	
Copyright © 2017 by Kevin Everett FitzMaurice	https://kevinfitzmaurice.com

C2: 2 Keys to Maturity

> A man's maturity consists in having found again the seriousness one had as a child, at play.
>
> —Friedrich Nietzsche

As you read this chapter, notice how all the keys to maturity are dependent upon emotional responsibility. For example, you will not be able to run your own mind if you are not responsible for how you feel. Maturity is dependent upon emotional maturity, and emotional maturity is dependent upon emotional responsibility.

Likewise, the keys to maturity are dependent upon emotional maturity, and emotional maturity is dependent upon emotional responsibility. Hence, emotional responsibility should be your primary focus for developing greater maturity.

This chapter organizes many keys to maturity under two headings: "Run Your Own Mind" and "Run Your Own Self". The following chapter covers additional keys to maturity some of which might have been collected here as well. And what are "keys" for you in the sense of understanding maturity? Your keys to maturity are the concepts and ideas that you find engaging, stimulating, and worth pursuing. Enough "keys" are offered for you to find the ones that fit for your journey to maturity. No need to purse them all.

1. Run Your Own Mind

> The relish of good and evil depends in a great measure upon the opinion we have of them.
>
> —Michel Eyquem de Montaigne

Learning to run your own mind is one of the keys to understanding the nature of maturity. When outside forces determine what you think, then outside forces are running your mind, not you.

REBT

Rational Emotive Behavior Therapy (REBT) teaches that you do not feel anything about an event until you interpret that event. And, since you are free to interpret events any way that you want, you are responsible for the feelings that result from your interpretations. REBT theory goes on to state that your beliefs determine your interpretations and therefore your feelings—hence, if you change your basic beliefs, then your feelings will automatically change.

In practice, REBT is typically an attack on irrational beliefs that cause undue upset and also a strengthening of rational beliefs that lead to greater adaptability. REBT literature defines irrational and rational beliefs and provides a list of common irrational beliefs. (For an example list, see "11 Irrational Beliefs" in chapter *Assorted Additions*. For more on REBT and irrational beliefs, see *A New Guide to Rational Living, Third Edition* by Albert Ellis and Robert A. Harper.)

Are you willing to recognize your responsibility for your beliefs and interpretations that cause your feelings, and then to act accordingly? Even when you feel hurt or angry? Even when you want to blame others?

Here is one example of the power that interpretation has to color how you view and feel about events: You are driving down the highway, and another car speeds dangerously past your car. You can think, "What an idiot. Who do they think they are, treating me like a nobody or a nothing?" and feel hurt and angry. Or, you can think, "I hope they make it to their emergency on time," and feel concerned and calm.

General Semantics

General Semantics has a similar set of suggested coping strategies or techniques that Attribution Theory's suggestions might in fact be based upon. Conversely, REBT does give General Semantics credit for being part of the foundation of REBT theory and practice, along with Stoic and Buddhist philosophies.

Unfortunately, General Semantics is neither as well-known nor as studied as it deserves to be. General Semantics is the Western way of understanding and realizing Zen perception and experience—that is, you experience from inner silence instead of from inner thinking.

General Semantics teaches four techniques or principles—known as *extensional versus intensional orientations, non-allness, indexing,* and *dating*—that are similar to Attribution Theory's internal, unstable, and specific techniques or principles.

To use an *extensional orientation* is to view the world from an objective perspective, such as how things or events relate to a meaningless void.

To take an *intensional orientation* is to view the world from a subjective perspective, such as how things or events relate to your feelings, opinions, experiences, and ego.

Being aware if you are thinking extensionally or intensionally can help you to become aware of the attributions you make to internal or external causes, both for yourself and others.

The practice of *non-allness* is used to keep you from overgeneralization, dogma, or certainty and, instead, to move you to embrace chance, probability, or predictability. Non-allness can be used to realize that life is unstable, changing, and varying; hence, life won't always be as bad or good as it once was.

Indexing can be used to make events and experiences specific to a time and place rather than general to all times and places, by organizing and categorizing events with similar events and experiences to foster taking perspective and gaining psychological distance from each event or experience.

Dating can be used to make events and experiences specific or individual rather than general or global, by dating events to specific times and places so that single events are prevented from representing all times or all places related to an event.

(See *Science and Sanity: An Introduction to Non-Aristotelian Systems and General Semantics, Fourth Edition* by Alfred Korzybski. FitzMaurice's book that is most concerned with topics related to General Semantics is *We're All Insane! Second Edition*.)

Attribution Theory

Attribution Theory comes from Social Psychology. Attribution Theory is concerned with how we attribute the causes of our own and others' actions or feelings. What do you believe causes people's actions? Why do different people react differently to the same event or circumstances? To what do you attribute the variety and variability of human actions and reactions to similar stimuli?

For example, according to Attribution Theory, you tend to attribute the bad actions of others to internal causes and your own bad actions to external causes. You might think, "There must be something wrong with them, for them to act so stupidly," versus, "I only acted stupidly because I had a really stressful day."

Attribution Theory suggests that a mature attribution style is *internal, unstable,* and *specific*. This means you realize that control, choices, or options originate internally (inside yourself, not externally); principles or traits that lead to errors can be instantly changed (causes are not stable or stuck); and errors are specific to the situation in which they occur (not general to all situations).

This mature style is believed to provide for a saner and more satisfying life. (See *Social Psychology: The Second Edition* by Roger William Brown.)

Do you think we should be fair, realistic, or consistent in how we attribute motivation or cause to the actions of self and others? Is it more beneficial to blame or to take responsibility? It is more beneficial to damn others or to show compassion for others? Are people different, or is there only one human nature?

Internal Locus of Control

In different psychologies, varying importance is placed on where you put or presume your or "the" locus (location or seat) of control to be located.

That is, do you essentially have an internal or an external locus of control? At one extreme is internal locus of control—for example, people who believe all is chaos and chance and you can therefore make your life whatever you want. At the other extreme is external locus of control—for example, people who believe all is fated or predestined to go according to some plan or pattern.

Do you see yourself as controlling events or events as controlling you? Does life control your life, or do you control your life? In what circumstances do you see the locus of control as within yourself, and in what circumstances do you see the locus of control as outside of yourself? Is there the possibility for a balanced view of locus of control that would both give you control in some circumstances and give life control in some circumstances?

A related concept is determinism versus volition. For instance, Sigmund Freud and B. F. Skinner favored determinism, while Albert Ellis favored volition. For an understanding of a method of processing other than dualism (conflict, dialectics, opposites), see "5 Thinking Positions Scale for Maturity" in *C8: Assorted Additions*.

Inner-Directed Personality

A perhaps existential concept is the *inner-directed* personality versus the *outer-directed* personality. Do you basically find motivation, approval, and support from within yourself (from internal ideals or values) or from outside of yourself (from laws, others' opinions, or possessions)?

How do people learn to be an outer-directed personality, and how can people learn to seek direction from within? Is it possible to have motivation, approval, and support from within and without? When is it best to have internal direction, and when is it best to accept external direction? Can you balance both internal and external, so that they support each other? Or must the inner-directed person always find himself or herself at odds with the world, as history so often demonstrates in the cases of great talent or genius?

How many inner-directed people have been crushed by the weight of the critical conformists in religion, science, art, and government? Dare you sing your own song and risk losing external support and finding external enemies when you sing?

2. Run Your Own Self

> The individual has always had to struggle to keep from being overwhelmed by the tribe. If you try it, you will be lonely often, and sometimes frightened. But no price is too high to pay for the privilege of owning yourself.
>
> —Friedrich Nietzsche

Learning to run your own self is one of the keys to understanding the nature of maturity. Don't blamers and whiners sound immature? Don't people act like irresponsible children when they think that others are controlling them?

Self-Ownership

> Responsibility is the high price of self-ownership.
>
> —Eli J. Schleifer

Who owns your self? Who determines your self? How much are you in possession of your self? Is self-ownership possible, or must you serve the needs of your community first? Are you going to serve an ideal purpose with your life, or are you going to serve your culture, conditioning, and community with your life?

Your answers depend both on how much responsibility you take for yourself, and on how much responsibility you give or blindly surrender to others. How much of your self do you possess with your own ideals? How much of your self do your family, friends, job, possessions, ethnicity, culture, religion, government, and education possess with their ideals and demands?

Can you tell the difference between experiences of self that come from within and experiences of self that come from without? How?

The great quest to find the self, to be a self, or to know yourself can be understood as an attempt to discover what the self wants or feels without the interference of conditioning or environment.

Is such a state desirable? Is it possible to live condition-free in society, or must one be a hermit? If you discover yourself as a hermit, then will you lose yourself if you return to society? Can you be sure that you have your self only in relationship to others? Or is your self something that works wherever self is?

Can the self be lost, or can the self only be surrendered or suppressed? Is personality just a covering for the self, a way to hide from your self? Is self-ownership worth disowning all the false selves that you have inherited or created? Is your self nothing more than a Frankenstein monster created from the dead parts of other people? Can self be reduced to things and thoughts for the sake of the machinations and manipulations of ego and self-esteem?

Self-Reliance

> Know thyself.
>
> —Inscription over the entrance of the temple of Apollo at Delphi

Humanists and philosophers write about *self-reliance,* about independence from society and the mob, and of seeking strength from within. If you choose self-reliance, does that mean you will be alone? Do you want to be alone? Can you be self-reliant in relationships?

Does self-reliance mean that you rely on your own internal ideals as opposed to the ideals of others? Does self-reliance mean that you can never seek advice or support? Is it possible to know when to rely on internal values and when to seek higher values? Is there a continuum from independence to dependence, for rational or pragmatic self-reliance?

An effective understanding of self-reliance is that you rely on your own experiences before you rely on the experiences of others or on authorities. (For more on self-reliance, see the writings of Henry David Thoreau.) (For an essay on why to avoid groupthink, read *The Crowd Is Untruth* by Søren Kierkegaard.)

Personal Autonomy

> The longest journey is the journey inward.
>
> —Dag Hammarskjöld

Personal autonomy is the subject of many disciplines and is simply self-rule as opposed to being ruled by your conditioning, culture, or environment. Are your decisions based upon your own wants and needs, or are your decisions based upon the needs and wants that have been inflicted upon you as your own?

Just what governs you? Where is the governing process in you, and how did it get there? Have your intentions ever been questioned, and should they be? Are you only serving some conditioning that works to promote some phony religion or greedy culture? Who is in charge of your life? Where did your intentions come from, and where are they leading you? Do you assume your motivations are your own?

It is unlikely that you have ever known anyone who has had an original thought about religion, science, or government. Yet, everyone you know acts as if his or her thinking is his or her own instead of just a conditioned response. Is it time to examine the premises of your beliefs?

Centering

> Life inspires more dread than death—it is life which is the great unknown.
>
> —Emile M. Cioran

Centering is still another way of examining the self for maturity. The concept of centering has nothing to do with being self-centered; but, rather, refers to where your being—your consciousness—is located. Are you centered in your self?

Are you located in the center of your being? Or are you scattered about in people, places, things, tasks, and roles? Is your mind, attention, and awareness absorbed and stimulated by your environment? Or is your mind, attention, and awareness absorbed and stimulated by your internal ideals?

A consumer society conditions you to be centered in consuming stimulation in the form of consumable products, deadening media, disposable possessions, and social events. A person who is not centered is focused on their external life and being guided by fashions, political correctness, styles, and trends. A centered individual is focused on his or her internal life and being guided by his or her internal ideals.

Interestingly, Centering Prayer can be considered the Western tradition of meditation that is similar to many traditional forms of Eastern meditation.

Individualist versus Follower

> We grow shells to protect ourselves. Too often the shells become us.
>
> —Eli J. Schleifer

Political analysts talk of the individualist versus the follower, or independent thought versus groupthink. Is groupthink just another name for political correctness? Can you stand up to the crowd and have a different opinion? Can you be balanced in both individual and group perspectives?

Can you agree and disagree with the groups that you belong to? Must you chose to conform and completely follow some group or be rejected and despised by that group? Are there groups that will accept you with your differences? Must the choice be between follower or individualist? Or can you choose when to follow and when to stand alone?

Can you think outside of the box of your associations, clubs, or other memberships? How many individualists have been persecuted by governments, religions, scientific organizations, art authorities, or other calcified centers of society? Why must the individual historically be at odds with the group?

External Referenting

> There is but one cause of human failure. And that is man's lack of faith in his true Self.
>
> —William James

External referenting is another psychological concept that can be used to explore the issue of maturity. Do you refer to the outside or to the inside of yourself for your approval? Do you trust your own perceptions only if they are externally verified?

Does your meaning come from outside or inside yourself? Do you refer to self or others for your reality? Do you trust or value your own experience above the experience of any authority? Is your own experience the first and last test for what you accept and hold to be true? Do you refer to the experiences of your group or of yourself for your beliefs? Does political correctness outweigh your own experiences?

Is your experience so diluted with ego and social pressures that your experience is no longer genuinely your experience? Has your experience been corrupted to the point that your experience is no longer your reliable standard of measurement and comparison?

What can you do to return to your experiences the integrity they once had? What can you do to return to your ego-less experience as a reliable standard for truth?

C3: More Keys to Maturity

> Tragedy is in the eye of the observer, and not in the heart of the sufferer.
>
> —Emerson

To Thy Own Self Be True

> To thy own self be true.
>
> —William Shakespeare

> Maturity consists of no longer being taken in by one's self.
>
> —Kajetan Von Schlaggenberg

Do you lie to yourself about what you think and feel? Do you filter and suppress what you think and feel? How can you be honest with others if you are not honest with yourself? Are you willing to suffer ego pain from observing your internal processes as they are? Must you escape facing yourself because of the pain of inner ugliness? Can you cope when facing the dark side of human nature in yourself?

Are you honest with yourself about your intentions? For instance, when you respond sarcastically to someone, can you admit that your intention was to cause him or her ego pain (emotional hurt), either out of revenge or sadism? Can you admit to yourself when you lie, cheat, and steal?

If you are excusing, justifying, and rationalizing your immoral actions, then you are not being true to yourself. If you are not being true to yourself, then how can you be true to others or God?

Do you stand up for what you believe, or do you let peer pressure, political correctness, and mob pressure make a coward of you? Do you tolerate racist humor when you know it is immoral and destructive for all of humanity? Is there an ideal that is more important to you than your own life?

Can you keep peace with others and at the same time stick to your own principles? Are you able to allow others their own way and, at the same time, able to insist on your own way for yourself? Can you let others be wrong without having to prove them wrong? If you are not following your own ideals instead of some group ideals, then you are not being true to yourself.

Being true to yourself involves two principles:

1. Tell yourself the truth about your intentions.

2. Stand up for and follow your highest ideals.

Dependent Feelings & Dependent Behaviors

> When we cannot be delivered from ourselves, we delight in devouring ourselves.
>
> —Emile M. Cioran

Stanton Peele in his seminal book, *Love and Addiction,* explores the direct relationship between dependent feelings and dependent behaviors. In his book, addiction is correctly understood as a problem of emotional dependency or emotional immaturity. Perhaps the most important insight of the book is that when you become dependent on others and things, then you can become an addictive personality.

Who and what do you rely upon? Who or what is best to rely upon? Is it possible to find a balance for what you are dependent upon? Can people be reliably depended upon for your best interests? Can people be reliably depended upon for support and encouragement? Can people be reliably depended upon for helping you face the truth of your intentions?

Detachment

Al-Anon teaches the concept of *detachment* as a means to disengage your feelings about self from the actions and feelings of others. When your feelings about self no longer depend on the feelings of someone else, then you have detached from that person.

Detachment does not mean not having feelings. Detachment has nothing to do with being frozen, coldness, deadness, numbness, or shutting down. Quite the contrary, detachment allows you to admit and experience more feelings without filters or suppression. Detachment means that your ego or self-esteem is no longer attached to your body, experiences, possessions, or to the opinions of others.

- Detachment is freedom to feel.
- Detachments means making it not about you.
- Detachment is keeping your identity out of it whatever it is.

Some twelve-step programs deal specifically with emotional dependency—for example, Emotions Anonymous and Adult Children of Alcoholics. At least one twelve-step program focuses on love or romance addiction: Sex and Love Addicts Anonymous.

Does your happiness depend upon the happiness of those around you? Do your feelings depend upon the feelings of those around you? Does your approval come from within or from others? Can you detach your identity from family, friends, and your group memberships? Does being detached make you a robot or more capable of feeling freely? Is detachment deadness or openness? Is detachment the path to shallowness of feeling or to infinite depth of feeling?

When you are detached, then you have no ego to defend or protect. Without an ego to defend or protect, you have greater freedom to experience and feel. Without an ego to defend or protect, you can respond maturely (acceptance, forgiveness, understanding) in situations in which you previously responded immaturely (blaming, damning, whining).

Codependency

Codependency is a concept in the field of addictions that is defined in various ways. Codependency is most often concerned with emotional dependency, enmeshment, and boundary problems.

Do you live your life through others? Do you feel good only when you can make others feel good or better? Do you feel compelled to rescue people rather than to let them struggle towards maturity? Do you respect people enough to let them learn to take care of themselves? Are you playing martyr to please your ego while pretending it is to please those you serve? *Do you need to try to help people—while keeping them helpless, so you can feel superior to them?*

Unfortunately, if parents, counselors, psychiatrists, and social workers were honest with themselves about their intentions and results, then many would have to answer "yes" to that last question. (For more on codependency, see *Codependent No More* by Melody Beattie.)

Boundaries & Limits

The concepts of boundaries and limits can be another helpful way to explore maturity. Personal boundaries can be considered the beginning and end of your personal and social space for life. Personal limits can be considered the finite amount of energy, time, and resources that you have to share or contribute.

Are your boundaries so rigid that you become a closed system, wherein nothing can enter? Are your boundaries so permeable that you become an open system that anything can enter?

Think of your body and its immune system. Your body must allow in air, water, and food. But your body must also keep out infection, injury, and disease. Therefore, your body must be both an open and a closed system, depending on what needs to come into the system and what needs to be kept or kicked out of the system. Can you have boundaries for your life that seek out good influences and keep out bad influences? Can you forgive someone but still keep him or her out of your life, knowing he or she is a bad influence or a continual source of the negative?

Do you know where your emotional boundaries begin and end? Do the feelings of others easily enter you to become your own? Do others' opinions of you easily enter you to become your own, whether or not you want them to? Do you have definite identity boundaries between yourself and others—including between yourself and significant others?

Are you looking for someone who will live inside your boundaries with you? That is what many think romantic love looks like, but that is enmeshment, not romance. Enmeshment is when two or more people form one ego. An entire family can be enmeshed or have what Murray Bowen called an *undifferentiated ego mass*.

Can you say "no" to charity, helping, or service, based on knowing your limits? Can you say "yes" to charity, helping, or service, based on knowing your limits? Do you know your limits to providing care for others versus providing self-care so that you might be able to care for others?

On airplanes, the stewards tell you to put on your own oxygen mask first, before trying to help anyone else with their oxygen masks. That is the way life works. Take care of yourself first so that you might be able to take care of others next. Despite magical positive thinking, you have limited capabilities, energy, time, and resources. Make sure to serve first things first so that you can serve better and more for others afterward.

> Physician, heal thyself.
>
> —Luke 4:23

Systems Theory

Systems Theory, as developed in the Circumplex Model of family systems, models basic family interaction patterns or styles. The two major scales are adaptability and cohesion. At the low end of the cohesion scale, we find families that are emotionally disengaged (no feelings are based on the group); and at the high end of the scale, we find families that are emotionally enmeshed (all feelings are based on the group).

Of course, healthy families are not found at the extremes but, rather, somewhere in the middle. Are you able to have both individual-based and group-based feelings, or mostly only one or the other?

Systems Theory uncovers an all too common way to maintain emotional immaturity: *triangulation*. Compare triangulation to the "Blame Game" in chapter *C1: What is Maturity?*, the Karpman Drama Triangle, and the more advanced and comprehensive diagrams in *Games Ego Plays*. For example, one marriage partner enters therapy, and his or her therapist becomes his or her advocate, triangulates with him or her, and encourages him or her to get a divorce as a way out of his or her troubles. The therapy client gets a divorce, but then remarries into a similar relationship. Why? Because he or she never worked on his or her own choices, conditioning, emotional maturity, habits, identity, intentions, interpretations, thinking, and life script issues as the actual cause of his or her troubles.

(An easy introductory text to family systems is *Family Communication: An Integrated Approach* by Evelyn Sieburg. Some might prefer *The Theory and Technique of Family Therapy* by Charles P. Barnard and Ramon G. Corrales.)

Are you willing to examine your interaction style for its destructive tendencies? Or will you continue to immaturely see others as causing all of your problems? There are plenty of therapists willing to take your money in order to support and rationalize your view that you are a victim of others, whether or not you actually are a victim of anyone other than yourself. Yes, most people are their own victims; however, real perpetrators do still exist.

Creativity

Creativity in the individual is both as pure and as powerful as the individual's thought is free from dependence or reliance upon others. In both the arts and the sciences, such freedom of expression has historically put original thinkers at odds with their contemporaries.

Are you free from the influence of others to the point of originality? Most of us can only add variation or evolution to an existing idea, something that is not revolutionary thinking. Most of us are so bound because of our conditioning, our need for group approval, and our ego demands for pride that stems from "knowing better than" others.

Standing against the world has a price on your mind, body, and relationships. Many have escaped the pressure by running to drugs or alcohol. Many have gone insane from the pressure. Many have become ill from the pressure. Many have been made social outcasts by the mob. Many have been killed by the mob.

A historical example is the life of Søren Kierkegaard. Kierkegaard stood alone against both the secular and the religious worlds, and as a result of that stress, one day he dropped dead in the street.

A recent example is the life of Steve Jobs. Unfortunately, the negative stress of standing against universal stupidity was not just let out in occasional angry outbursts; the negative stress was also carried by his body and so it killed him. Companies like Google and Microsoft still don't understand Job's main message that "Simple is superior."

Google and Microsoft most likely never will understand, because Google and Microsoft are run by technocrats and bureaucrats whose job security and existence depends upon things not being simple. Change is more likely to come from websites that do computer and technology reviews when they stop hiring out-of-touch techies and start using computer-illiterate consumers to review new computer and technology products. The average consumer no more wants to modify his or her computer than he or she wants to modify his or her car. The computer hobbyist period is long gone, and the "appliance" computer dream of Steve Jobs is upon us.

Solitude

> As for solitude, I cannot understand how certain people seek to lay claim to intellectual stature, nobility of soul and strength of character, yet have not the slightest feeling for seclusion; for solitude, I maintain, when joined with a quiet contemplation of nature, a serene

> and conscious faith in creation and the Creator, and a few vexations from outside is the only school for a mind of lofty endowment.
>
> —Goethe

Is solitude one of your needs? If you cannot stand your own company, then why should anyone else stand your company? If you don't like to be alone with you, then why should anyone else want to be alone with you? If you don't make it a point to spend time alone with yourself, then why should anyone else make it a point to spend time with you? If your only value exists in the company of others, then how real is that value?

Solitude is the best way to contemplate, pray, and meditate. Solitude will bring you face-to-face with yourself. Solitude will bring you face-to-face with your negative and positive intentions. Solitude is scary when your ego is weak, because solitude offers no escape from self-examination. Solitude is just as necessary for self-knowledge as social relationships are. You can learn about yourself only through both solitude and social relationships. Solitude teaches about internal relationships, and social relationships teach about external relationships. The self is revealed in both internal and external relationship, and right self-knowledge is acquired from direct experience.

> Alone, even doing nothing, you do not waste your time. You do, almost always, in company. No encounter with yourself can be altogether sterile: Something necessarily emerges, even if only the hope of some day meeting yourself again.
>
> —Emile M. Cioran

True Strength

> To live with fear and not be afraid is the final test of maturity.
>
> —Edward Weeks

Loudmouths, tough guys, and those who think they have to fight are the weakest of all people. The truth is that strength is exactly the opposite of what the macho or the machismo code defines as strength.

The person who is responsible for his or her own feelings is the strongest. The person who can be insulted by anyone—or who has to fight to save face—is the weakest.

It does not matter if the costume of the day is that of a cowboy, detective, gang member, samurai, soldier, sports player, spy, superhero, or what have you. The weakest are made to feel by others simply by what others say to them. To prove that they don't have to feel that way, the weakest respond like lizards and fight. The macho personality is the weakest and most immature personality popularly accepted: None other is so easy to control, predict, or manipulate on an emotional level as the primitive macho type is.

The strong are able to turn the other cheek. The strongest was willing to be crucified for His beliefs without complaint or defense.

Adults use the expression, "It takes a bigger man to walk away [from a fight or argument]," to show that the person in control of his or her own feelings is the bigger or stronger person. Similarly, the expression, "It takes a big man to admit when he is wrong," refers to the fact that the person whose feelings are not dependent upon the input of others is more in possession of themselves (bigger), and thus has more strength to be able to admit failings or feelings.

Who decides what actions you will take: the thoughts and words of others, or your own ideals?

Think of it this way: Does a grown man have to punch and kick back when he is punched and kicked by a four-year-old boy? No. Why not? Because the punching and kicking that a four-year-old boy can do to a grown man is inconsequential and can therefore be ignored.

It is the same with emotional violence and insults. If you are centered in yourself and strong in self-ownership, then any emotional violence or insults directed towards you simply reflect on the emotional weakness, immaturity, insecurity, and lack of intelligence of your attackers.

Immunity to Insults

> When, therefore, anyone provokes you, be assured that it is your own opinion that provokes you.
>
> —Epictetus

> No one can make you feel inferior without your consent.
>
> —Eleanor Roosevelt

Children use the expression, "Sticks and stones will break my bones, but words will never hurt me," to show invulnerability in the face of verbal attack. Their invulnerability comes from their reliance (hopefully) on self to determine how they will feel.

Do insults wound you? Do you feel a need to respond to insults? Do you have to own the attacks that others make on you? Can you look upon people who resort to personality attacks as pitiful and weak-minded? Can you feel sorry for people who lack the intelligence to form an argument and hence must resort to name-calling, emotional violence, and put-downs? Do you understand that the *ad hominen* argument is known to be a logical fallacy?

> Remember that the ruling facility is invincible, when self-collected it is satisfied with itself.
>
> —Marcus Aurelius

Culture & Maturity

> Maturing is the transcendence from environmental support to self-support.
>
> —Fritz (Frederick S.) Perls

If it is known in various ways that the key to growing up, to being mature, to being responsible depends entirely on emotional responsibility, why does our culture promote emotional immaturity? It promotes emotional immaturity with its everyday acceptance of phrases such as: "You made me… [insert feeling word, such as *mad*]," "She made me…," "They make me…," "It made me…," "That makes me…," etc.

The simple truth is that no one ever has or ever will *make* you feel anything. People can make your body feel something through physical contact, but people are not capable of controlling your mind or heart through similar direct contact. Others may and do provide situations or stimuli that you might feel compelled to respond to. But the choice to respond at all—and the choice of how to respond—are both always yours, as are your resulting feelings regarding your choices about that experience.

Our culture also promotes dependent and symbiotic relationships in the name of love. This is done most obviously and consistently through country and western music, but it is also continually done through rock 'n' roll, romantic movies, romance novels, and soap operas. All the various forms of Western media are used in some way to promote dependent relationships as the fulfillment of true love.

(For some interesting critiques on the influences of culture that cause and maintain immaturity see: chapters thirteen through fifteen of *On Becoming a Person* by Carl R. Rogers, chapter three of *The Art of Loving* by Erich Fromm, chapter five of *Co-Dependence Misunderstood-Mistreated* by Anne Wilson Schaef, *Love and Addiction* by Stanton Peele, *The Politics of Experience* by R. D. Laing, *The Manufacture of Madness* by Thomas S. Szasz, and *Think on These Things* by J. Krishnamurti.)

Why Immature?

My one fear is that I will not be worthy of my sufferings.

—Dostoyevsky

Buttons Pushed?

If people "push your buttons" or "get to you," it is not because you let them—you cannot give people power over your mind and heart—it is because you did it to yourself in their name. Why do we push our own buttons and blame others for it? Why do we do that with some people and not others? The reasons can vary, but some common ones are:

- That person looks, sounds, or acts as a parental figure did.

- That person reminds us of a significant other.

- That person uses body language, particularly facial expressions and body stances, as someone else did in a previous emotional game.

- We think that person knows who we are.

Other reasons for relating to others immaturely include:

- The game is our habit.

- We are in a weakened position because we are not taking care of basic needs such as eating, sleeping, exercising, making contact, getting recognition, sharing feelings, and contributing to our community.

• We know how to relate that way, so it is safer or easier than other unknown ways of relating with people.

• We like the drama and excitement of the game.

Unpredictable Effects

There are no biological or scientific cause-and-effect reasons for feeling one way in any particular situation as opposed to feeling another way. Therefore, people have and will continue to have varying reactions to the same situations. Over time, even the same person will often react differently to the same situations. Human emotions are more of a choice than a reaction, unlike most physical responses to stimuli. For instance, if you slap a stranger for no apparent reason:

• He or she might act shocked and perplexed.

• He or she might ask you why you did that.

• He or she might beg you not to slap them again.

• He or she might beg your forgiveness.

• He or she might call the police.

• He or she might cry.

- He or she might enjoy the slap and ask you to slap him or her again.

- He or she might feel angry and plan to revenge himself or herself on you.

- He or she might feel anxious and afraid that you will do worse things.

- He or she might ignore you.

- He or she might laugh at you and call you names.

- He or she might run away.

- He or she might slap you back.

- He or she might think he or she deserves the slap and wait to be slapped again.

Clearly, the individual's interpretation of the slap has more effect on how he or she feels than the slap itself does. Obviously, you did not cause him or her to feel the way he or she chose to feel, but you did provide a negative stimulus for him or her to have feelings about.

> That which is evil to thee and harmful
> has its foundation only in the mind.
>
> —Marcus Aurelius

C4: 6 Levels of Emotional Maturity

> Men are disturbed not by things, but by the view which they take of them.
>
> —Epictetus

In this chapter, the six levels of emotional maturity are presented from lowest to highest. However, the interdependence of the levels of emotional maturity makes listing them from lowest to highest somewhat artificial. Feel free to reorder the list as suits your needs. The six levels are emotional responsibility, emotional honesty, emotional openness, emotional assertiveness, emotional understanding, and emotional detachment.

Table: 6 Levels of Emotional Maturity

6 Levels of Emotional Maturity	
1	Emotional Responsibility
2	Emotional Honesty
3	Emotional Openness
4	Emotional Assertiveness
5	Emotional Understanding
6	Emotional Detachment
Copyright © 2017 by Kevin Everett FitzMaurice https://kevinfitzmaurice.com	

Level 1 of Emotional Maturity

Emotional Responsibility

When a person reaches level one of emotional maturity, then he or she realizes that he or she can no longer view his or her emotional states as the responsibility of external forces such as people, places, things, forces, fate, and spirits. He or she learns to drop expressions from his or her speech that show disownership of feelings and a helpless or victim attitude towards his or her feelings. Expressions such as: "They made me feel…," "It made me feel…," "I made them feel…," and any others that denote external emotional responsibility are first changed into *I statements* as opposed to "You…" or blaming statements. For example, common expressions are changed from, "You make me so mad when you do that," to, "I feel mad when you do that because…."

People at this level of emotional maturity regularly use the following two expressions:

- "When you did that, I felt …, because I thought it meant …."

- "When that happened, I felt …, because I interpreted it to mean …."

As time and maturity advance, the emotionally responsible begin to use even more accurate statements that inhibit the Blame Game such as:

- "I chose to feel … when you or I did that, because I thought it meant …."

- "I choose to feel … whenever that happens, because I choose to think it means …."

- "I chose to feel … when he, she, or it did that, because I chose to think it means …."

- "I am in the habit of choosing to feel … whenever my or your [mother, father, sister, brother, etc.] says anything to me, because I think it means …."

Level 2 of Emotional Maturity

> The greatest weapon against stress is our ability to choose one thought over another.
>
> —William James

Emotional Honesty

Emotional honesty concerns the willingness of a person to know and own his or her feelings. This is a necessary step to self-acceptance and self-understanding. The issue of resistance to self-discovery is dealt with at this level. Resistance issues stem from the person's conscious and unconscious fears of dealing directly with the critical voices he or she hears inside his or her mind. Such fears are based upon the emotional pain that ego, self-esteem, and self-talk have inflicted in the past.

When people don't learn emotional coping skills, they generally lose most interactions with their internal adversary, internal critic, negative self-talk, or hyperactive conscience. Therefore, people's fears of emotional honesty are based upon past ego pain from being internally judged as worse than, lower than, or inferior to others. People at this level of emotional honesty know how to choose to feel so that they can keep from being hurt. They also know how to choose to not interact with their inner accusers by using ignoring, distracting, or redirecting techniques. (For more on ignoring, distracting, and redirecting techniques, see FitzMaurice's *Garden*.)

The realization of the old maxim, "To thine own self be true," is the primary goal at this level of maturity. In this context, the meaning of the maxim is that you are always true to what you feel. At this level of emotional maturity, you do not hide, stuff, suppress, or repress what you feel, but you honestly experience what you feel. You are at least honest with yourself about how you really feel despite what you are supposed to feel. However, this honesty in no way requires you to act the way that you feel. In fact, acting the opposite of how you feel is one strategy for changing how you feel.

As a secondary goal on this level, people learn to locate others with whom they can safely share their real feelings, their real selves, in an accepting and supporting manner. At this level, the work is also begun to never again accept self as your behaviors or experiences. If you act like a dog forever, you will still never become a dog. Similarly, you will never become stupid from acting stupid. But you might want to focus on switching your stupid thinking for more realistic and effective thinking, behaviors, and results.

> We are born to Exist, not to know, to be,
> not to assert ourselves.
>
> —Emile M. Cioran

Level 3 of Emotional Maturity

> Why should we think upon things that
> are lovely? Because thinking determines
> life. It is a common habit to blame life
> upon the environment. Environment

modifies life but does not govern life.
The soul is stronger than its
surroundings.

—William James

Emotional Openness

This level of maturity concerns a person's willingness to share and skills in sharing his or her feelings in an appropriate manner and at appropriate times. Persons at this level experience and learn the value of ventilating feelings to let feelings go, and also the dangers involved in hiding feelings from self and others.

Self-disclosure is the important issue at this level of emotional maturity. Yet, self-disclosure will never be as important as the willingness of the person to be open to experiencing all of his or her feelings as they arise without the critical voices he or she hears inside trying to change, control, or condemn those feelings. The dangers of suppressing feelings and the value inherent in exploring all feelings and allowing them internal expression are investigated further over time at this level.

It is important to note that the ventilation of feelings has to be done correctly. If it is not your intention to let go of a feeling when you are ventilating that feeling, then you will feed and reinforce that feeling. Ventilating feelings can be destructive and counterproductive, or ventilating feelings can be freeing and open up your self to better options and choices.

At this level of emotional maturity, a person has the openness and freedom to experience any emotion without the need or compulsion to suppress or repress it. The suppression and repression of emotions is to protect the ego from harm and to protect the self from the ego pain that comes when the ego is harmed.

- Express to let pass.
- Share to let go.
- Stop stewing and start swimming.
- Ventilate to detach.

Level 4 of Emotional Maturity

> The greatest discovery of my generation is that a human being can alter his life by altering his attitudes of mind.
>
> —William James

Emotional Assertiveness

A person at this level of work enters a new era of positive self-expression. The primary goal here is to be able to ask for and to receive the nurturing that he or she needs and wants—first from self, and then from others.

He or she asserts his or her emotional needs in all of his or her relationships, if it is safe to do so. As a secondary goal, he or she also learns how to express any feeling appropriately in any situation. (For example, how to express a feeling without aggressive or manipulative overtones.)

A person at this level of emotional maturity makes time for his or her feelings—he or she prizes and respects those feelings. Such people understand the connections between suppressed feelings, negative stress, and illness.

Some actions that can be characterized as emotional assertiveness include:

- Asking for alone time to contemplate, meditate, and pray.

- Asking for encouragement to complete a task or to achieve a goal.

- Asking for help to grieve a loss.

- Asking for time and space alone to process feelings.

• Asking for understanding and compassion for some unpleasant feelings.

• Asking to be heard out without advice or judgment.

• Being able to accept compliments with a simple, "Thank you."

• Being able to accept thanks with a simple, "You are welcome."

• Expressing what you are feeling while giving the other person permission to feel differently.

• Expressing what you are feeling without requiring others to understand or appreciate your feelings.

• Informing others that you are feeling vulnerable and may react poorly to additional stress or to confrontation for a while.

• Letting someone know you love and care about them in a non-sexual and safe way.

• Offering congratulations to others for their achievements.

• Rewarding positive social behaviors with approval and support.

• Telling someone that you think what he or she did was smart, timely, or important.

Self-Concept: The Enemy Within

Levels five and six of emotional maturity were originally covered in the book *Self-Concept: The Enemy Within*. For your benefit, we have included levels five and six from *Self-Concept: The Enemy Within* in all editions since the third edition of *The Secret of Maturity*. However, some of the ideas contained in levels five and six might be missed without reading or understanding *Self-Concept: The Enemy Within*, which is now out of print. Instead, please consider reading FitzMaurice's book *Ego*.

Level 5 of Emotional Maturity

Emotional Understanding

Persons on this level of emotional maturity understand the actual cause-and-effect processes of emotional responsibility and emotional irresponsibility. Self-concepts and self-images are understood to be "the" problem interfering with emotional responsibility. Such a person realizes that it is not possible to have a so-called good self-concept or self-image without a complementary bad self-concept or self-image.

Because of the nature of knowledge and the formation of self-concepts and self-images, such people experience firsthand the fact that all self-concepts and self-images contain their opposites. Knowing that one half of some self-concept duality is still active inside him or her even if he or she hides it in darkness (unconsciousness), he or she begins to regularly leap beyond the pitfalls of self-concepts, self-images, and self-constructs. This knowledge of the unity of the opposites (of self-concepts and of knowledge) is applied daily to new situations. (For more on the unity of the opposites, read *We're All Insane, Second Edition*. To move beyond duality to triality, read *World Within: The Inner Life*.)

Other understandings at this level include the following:

1. Attempts to capture a moment of self can only kill the self, because the self is a living process and not knowledge or memory.

2. To reduce self to knowledge is literally to kill the self.

3. Either one has his or her self and is alive and experiencing, or one has found his or her self as knowledge, lost his or her self, is dead, and is remembering, not experiencing.

By their very nature, self-concepts and self-images are always externally referenced, and therefore, they are the forever perfect targets and hooks for the "Blame Game" in

C1: What Is Maturity? Knowing that self-concepts and self-images are the only hooks that can be used in the Blame Game, people at this level of emotional responsibility remember to work on seeing their own self-concepts and self-images and finding release from them. Self-knowledge is used to free the self from self-concepts and self-images rather than to form more self-concepts and self-images to imprison the self in ever more complicated and devious ways.

The main work here is a total shift from identifying with any self-concepts or self-images to identifying only with the true or natural self as a host.

> Casting down imaginations, and every high thing that exalteth itself against the knowledge of God.
>
> —II Corinthians 10:5

> He that findeth his life shall lose it.
>
> —Matthew 10:39

Level 6 of Emotional Maturity

Emotional Detachment

At this level, the person lives without the burden and snare of self-concepts, self-images, self-constructs, group-concepts, social-concepts, and thing-concepts. Such a person is only aware of self as process, as a sensing being, as an experiencing being, as a living vessel, as unknowable and untrappable—because self is alive and not static or fixed.

Such a person has died to the life of self as self-concepts and self-images. True detachment from all self-concepts has occurred. Thus true detachment from others has also occurred, which means that absolute emotional responsibility has been achieved (actually rediscovered).

Not having self-concepts or self-images to defend or promote, this person can remain unaffected by the Blame Game. Not having self-concepts or self-images to defend or promote, this person can experience unconditional love for their enemies. (For a method and a plan for overcoming and reducing your ego, please read FitzMaurice's book *Ego*.)

> That every one of you should know how to posses his vessel in sanctification and honor.
>
> —I Thessalonians 4:4

C5: 2 Tests for Emotional Maturity

First Self-Test for Emotional Maturity

> The fault, Dear Brutus, is not in our stars;
> but in ourselves, that we are underlings.
>
> —William Shakespeare

Scoring for Emotional Maturity

Your total score indicates your place on a continuum based upon the six levels of emotional maturity. The higher your score, the higher your level of emotional maturity. However, this is not an inventory or measurement system that has itself been tested, validated, or verified. Therefore, the results should be used only as an indication and not as facts. Alternately, you can benefit from reading and thinking about the items without taking the test.

Be forewarned, there are some questions that will lower your score when you answer in favor of the mature style. This was done to urge you to think more about your answers. Your answers are numerical from one (1) to five (5). The numbers represent answers on the continuum in the table below.

This first test is shorter than the second test.

Table: Test Result Scores

LEVEL	Always	Often	Sometimes	Rarely	Never
1	1	2	3	4	5
2	1	2	3	4	5
3	1	2	3	4	5
4	1	2	3	4	5
5	1	2	3	4	5
6	1	2	3	4	5

Level 1 Items: Emotional Responsibility

Answer each question on a scale of 1 to 5, with 1 being the lowest and 5 being the highest.

1. How often do you think that the environment has a lot to do with your mood?

2. How often do you think that people cause your your attitude to change?

3. How often do you think that people's attitudes influence your feelings about yourself?

4. How often do you think that stress controls your feelings?

5. How often do you think that the economy has a lot to do with your attitude?

6. How often do you think that your boss or employer has a lot to do with your mood?

7. How often do you think that your coworkers have a lot to do with your mood?

8. How often do you think that your family has a lot to do with your mood?

9. How often do you think that your friends have a lot to do with your mood?

10. How often do you think that your health has a lot to do with your mood?

11. How often do you believe that people are "doing you in"?

12. How often do you say something like, "It made me mad"?

13. How often do you say something similar to, "I chose to get upset about it"?

14. How often do you say something similar to, "I really made them mad!"?

15. How often do you say something similar to, "I really upset myself about that!"?

16. How often do you say something similar to, "I'm having a bad day"?

17. How often do you say something similar to, "That upset me"?

18. How often do you say something similar to, "They pushed my buttons"?

19. How often do you say something similar to, "You really pissed me off!"?

20. How often do you think that what happens to you causes you to feel the way that you do?

Level 2 Items: Emotional Honesty

Answer each question on a scale of 1 to 5, with 1 being the lowest and 5 being the highest.

1. How often are you afraid to know what you are feeling?

2. How often are you unaware of what you are feeling?

3. How often do you admit to yourself that you have a negative feeling?

4. How often do you allow yourself to fully experience a negative feeling?

5. How often do you contain your feelings for the right time and place?

6. How often do you deny your feelings?

7. How often do you fight off a feeling?

8. How often do you seek someone caring enough to share your deep feelings with?

9. How often do you hide your feelings from coworkers?

10. How often do you hide your feelings from family?

11. How often do you hide your feelings from friends?

12. How often do you hide your feelings from others?

13. How often do you hide your feelings from yourself?

14. How often do you suppress your feelings?

15. How often do you tell others that they are wrong when they point out or claim that you are having some negative feeling such as anger or jealousy?

16. How often do you tell yourself that you really don't feel a certain way?

17. How often do you tell yourself that you shouldn't feel a certain way?

18. How often do you think it is bad to feel some negative feelings?

19. How often do you think you are bad for feeling some negative feeling?

Level 3 Items: Emotional Openness

Answer each question on a scale of 1 to 5, with 1 being the lowest and 5 being the highest.

1. How often do you face your mixed, multiple, or varied feelings about one topic?

2. How often do you follow a feeling to its natural end?

3. How often do you get to fully express your feelings to another person?

4. How often do you honor your feelings?

5. How often do you incubate your feelings?

6. How often do you journal about your feelings?

7. How often do you look for the right time and place to share your feelings?

8. How often do you make time to be with your feelings?

9. How often do you pursue your feelings to discover them fully?

10. How often do you share all of your feelings about one thing to someone?

11. How often do you talk out your feelings?

12. How often do you vent your feeling in order to let them go?

13. How often are you able to let your feelings go after fully expressing them?

14. How often do your feelings spontaneously arise in you?

Level 4 Items: Emotional Assertiveness

Answer each question on a scale of 1 to 5, with 1 being the lowest and 5 being the highest.

1. How often do you ask others to consider your feelings in their decision making?

2. How often do you ask others to nurture and care for your feelings?

3. How often do you ask yourself to nurture and care for your feelings?

4. How often do you encourage others to listen to your feelings?

5. How often do you express your anger in an assertive manner rather than an aggressive manner?

6. How often do you express your sadness in a sharing fashion rather than a blaming fashion?

7. How often do you find people to talk to who are interested in your feelings?

8. How often do you make the time and space to deal with your feelings?

9. How often do you spend time alone with yourself?

10. How often do you take your feelings into account before making decisions?

Level 5 Items: Emotional Understanding

Answer each question on a scale of 1 to 5, with 1 being the lowest and 5 being the highest.

1. How often are you aware of the duality of self-concepts to the point of seeing the absurdity in pursuing either side?

2. How often are you aware of your tendencies to emotional irresponsibility?

3. How often are you aware that people are trying to hook you into the Blame Game by getting you to compare yourself as self-concepts?

4. How often are you aware that the search to find self as something is the search to lose self?

5. How often are you aware that to reduce self to knowledge is to kill self?

6. How often are you aware that your attempts to capture self are really attempts to murder self?

7. How often do you become aware that you are hiding one half of the duality of self-esteem from yourself?

8. How often do you find release from your self-concepts, self-images, self-constructs, and social-constructs?

9. How often do you free yourself from your self-concepts and ego?

10. How often do you move your identity from the contents (thoughts in the mind) to the container (the mind itself)?

11. How often do you move your identity from your self-concepts to your real self as a host?

12. How often do you recognize that your self-concepts are at the root of your biggest problems?

Level 6 Items: Emotional Detachment

Answer each question on a scale of 1 to 5, with 1 being the lowest and 5 being the highest.

1. How often are you aware of yourself as a being rather than a doing?

2. How often do you feel at total peace with everyone?

3. How often do you feel compassion for those who are stuck in self-concept games?

4. How often do you feel no need to defend yourself when attacked?

5. How often do you feel unconditional love for everyone?

6. How often do you find it just silly to think of either yourself or others as self-concepts or self-images?

7. How often do you find yourself to be the unbegun, unformed, or uncarved inside?

8. How often do you pray for your enemies to be under God?

9. How often do you stay detached when others are doing their best to get you to play the Blame Game?

10. How often do you think that we all share the same one human nature?

11. How often do you think that we are all the same; therefore, to talk about anyone is to talk about yourself?

12. How often do you think, "There but for the grace of God go I!"?

Second Self-Test for Emotional Maturity

> Imaginary pains are by far the most real we suffer, since we feel a constant need for them and invent them because there is no way of doing without them.
>
> —Emile M. Cioran

This is another test designed to do the same thing as the previous test for emotional maturity only with different and more questions. You can read the test questions without taking the test and find plenty to think about.

Scoring for Emotional Maturity

The total score indicates your place on a continuum based on the six levels of emotional maturity. The higher your score, the higher your level of emotional maturity. However, this is not an inventory or measurement system that has itself been tested, validated, or verified. Therefore, the results should be used only as an indication and not as facts. Additionally, some levels have more items than other levels making comparisons between the levels artificial.

Be forewarned, there are some questions that will lower your score when you answer in favor of the mature style. This was done to urge you to think more about your answers. A perfect score is neither desirable nor possible. Your answers are numerical from one (1) to five (5). The numbers represent answers on the continuum in the table below.

This second test is longer than the first test.

Table: Test Result Scores

LEVEL	Always	Often	Sometimes	Rarely	Never
1	1	2	3	4	5
2	1	2	3	4	5
3	1	2	3	4	5
4	1	2	3	4	5
5	1	2	3	4	5
6	1	2	3	4	5

Level 1 Items: Emotional Responsibility

On a scale of 1 to 5, how often do you believe the following statements?

1. I am the victim of my behaviors.

2. I am the victim of my feelings.

3. I am the victim of my thoughts.

4. I avoid some of my family members to avoid feeling bad.

5. I believe that no one can make me feel hurt.

6. I believe that no one can make me glad.

7. I believe that no one can make me mad.

8. I believe that no one can make me sad.

9. I believe that no one can make me scared.

10. I can make people feel pretty comfortable.

11. I feel hurt when others do not do what I expect them to do.

12. I have often been let down by my friends.

13. I have the choice to set boundaries for my own behaviors.

14. I have the choice to set boundaries for my own feelings.

15. I have the choice to set boundaries for my own thoughts.

16. I know how to push other people's buttons.

17. If my friends stopped picking on me, then I could change.

18. If my friends stopped picking on me, then I would feel better.

19. If others would just treat me well, then I would never feel unhappy.

20. In my view, happiness mostly depends on how other people treat me.

21. It's my mother's fault that I'm an aggressive person.

22. My family can always make me feel bad.

23. My family is responsible for my bad manners.

24. Other people can never have power over my feelings.

25. Other people have power over my feelings.

26. Other people only have power over my feelings if I give it to them.

27. People who are emotional make me uncomfortable.

28. People won't allow me to live life the way I want to.

29. Some people can make me feel bad about myself no matter what I do.

30. When bad things happen to me it is because of other people.

31. When people I know well point out my faults I feel angry.

32. When people I know well point out my faults I feel hurt.

Level 2 Items: Emotional Honesty

On a scale of 1 to 5, how often do you believe the following statements?

1. I am aware of having subtle feelings.

2. I am not satisfied with my work unless some one else praises it.

3. I am pretty comfortable with allowing my feelings.

4. I am pretty comfortable with experiencing my feelings.

5. I am pretty comfortable with expressing my feelings.

6. I am still feeling guilty for some of my past wrongs.

7. I believe that since I am nice to people, they should be nice to me, too.

8. I can admit to feeling any way that I feel.

9. I can choose not to play mental-court games (for more information, see *Games Ego Plays)* over my feelings.

10. I can choose to feel another way if I do not like the way that I am feeling.

11. I can face whatever it is that I am feeling.

12. I can stand my ugly feelings.

13. I consciously choose beliefs that do not follow the patterns I was raised to follow.

14. I consciously choose values that do not follow the patterns I was raised to follow.

15. I consciously make choices that do not follow the patterns I was raised to follow.

16. I do not allow my feelings to be used as evidence to convict me of being bad.

17. I do not allow my feelings to be used in any internal-court games.

18. I do not blame life for how I feel.

19. I do not blame my friends for how I feel.

20. I do not blame my parents for how I feel.

21. I do not blame my spouse for how I feel.

22. I do not blame others for how I feel.

23. I do not have to hide my feelings from inner attacks.

24. I own my own feelings.

25. I recognize my feelings (anger, contempt, disgust, distress, fear, guilt, interest, joy, shame, surprise) when I have them.

26. I refuse to deny my feelings to myself.

27. I try to control other people so I can protect myself emotionally.

28. When I break a rule, I don't allow myself to feel bad, but I do consider the consequences.

29. While I might hide my feelings from others, I never hide my feelings from myself.

30. While I won't always tell others what I am feeling, I will always admit to myself what I am feeling.

Level 3 Items: Emotional Openness

On a scale of 1 to 5, how often do you believe the following statements?

1. I always respect other people's feelings.

2. I believe one of the best things in life is having someone with whom you can share all of your deepest feelings.

3. I can easily discuss my weaknesses as well as my strengths.

4. I can face my negative feelings with others in order to get past them.

5. I can share my feelings without blaming anyone for them.

6. I can share my feelings without damning anyone for them.

7. I can share my feelings without exaggerating them.

8. I can stick to the facts and keep my feelings to myself, if the situation calls for such a response.

9. I can tell by the situation that either it is or it is not beneficial to share my feelings.

10. I can tell when it is safe and when it is not safe to share my feelings.

11. I control my anger very well to the point of being able to act against it.

12. I do not believe in the open expression of love.

13. I do whatever I can to keep myself from crying in front of people.

14. I don't allow myself to feel sad or depressed.

15. I feel awkward when I hug someone of the same sex.

16. I feel awkward when I hug someone other than a close family member.

17. I find it difficult to show love to adults.

18. I find it easy to accept compliments.

19. I find it easy to compliment others.

20. I keep others guessing about how I am feeling.

21. I know that you cannot always safely or productively share your feelings.

22. I know when to share and when not to share my feelings.

23. I save my feelings for the right time and place to share them.

24. I seek out people and build relationships with people with whom I find it safe to share feelings.

25. I share my personal feelings with my close friends.

26. I work to create environments in which I can safely share my feelings.

27. I would rather not disclose my feelings to others.

28. It is difficult for me to accept love or admiration.

29. It is difficult for me to communicate negative feelings to others.

30. It is easy for me to communicate my positive feelings to someone.

31. It is hard for me to open up to others and share my deep feelings.

32. It's difficult for me to show my anger.

33. It's safer to keep my personal feelings to myself.

34. Just because I share my feelings, it does not mean that my thinking is not also important.

35. My close friends know just about everything I am feeling.

36. My feelings rise and fall like the tides of the ocean.

37. My feelings freely come and go.

38. My feelings are here today and gone tomorrow.

39. No matter which feelings I get, I do not hesitate to share them with my intimates.

40. When I share my feelings, they pass.

Level 4 Items: Emotional Assertiveness

On a scale of 1 to 5, how often do you believe the following statements?

1. I am a good parent for myself.

2. I am a good role model for parenting oneself.

3. I am able to ask for empathy.

4. I am able to ask for equal time in a conversation.

5. I am able to ask for listening time.

6. I am able to ask for love.

7. I am able to ask for nurturing.

8. I am able to ask for support.

9. I am able to ask myself to better care for me.

10. I am able to ask to be heard.

11. I am able to express my discontent with a friend when I think it's justified.

12. I am able to express my dreams to others.

13. I am able to express my hopes and ambitions to others.

14. I am able to express my values and ideals to others.

15. I am able to express my wants and desires to others.

16. I am able to see when I am not taking care of myself and then to start doing so again.

17. I avoid dealing with confrontations.

18. I can ask questions when I do not understand something.

19. I can endure hardship and suffering without emotional scarring.

20. I compliment people when I get the chance.

21. I do not baby myself, but I do take care of myself.

22. I do what people expect me to, even when I disagree with them.

23. I don't mind asking someone to repeat himself or herself, if I do not understand what he or she is saying.

24. I feel comfortable asking my boss for a raise or a promotion if I think I deserve it.

25. I feel comfortable saying, "No."

26. I feel free to politely voice my disagreements with people in authority.

27. I feel nervous when I talk to people that have any real position or authority.

28. I feel threatened when dealing with someone who is very aggressive.

29. I feel threatened when dealing with someone who is very assertive.

30. I feel threatened when dealing with someone who is very passive.

31. I feel uncomfortable pointing out to others that they have some food on their face or some dirt on their clothes.

32. I find it difficult to accept compliments without saying something negative about myself.

33. I have confidence in my abilities.

34. I make feeling time for myself.

35. I make space in my life for just sitting with my feelings.

36. I panic when I have to face someone who is angry.

37. I prefer not to criticize others, even if I am sure they are doing wrong.

38. If a friend woke me up late at night with an unimportant call, I could tell him or her that I was sleeping and prefer not to be called after a certain hour.

39. If I am overcharged in a store, I feel comfortable enough to bring it to the cashier's attention.

40. When a friend or colleague borrows something from me and forgets to return it, I hesitate to remind him or her.

41. When I feel angry, I can still choose to act assertively.

42. When I feel angry, I do not have to act angry.

43. When I feel angry, I can see that it is because my ego is hurt.

Level 5 Items: Emotional Understanding

On a scale of 1 to 5, how often do you believe the following statements?

1. I always choose my own attitude.

2. I can choose to feel differently whenever I want to.

3. I can objectively look at my feelings and follow them out to their natural end.

4. I can see when my feelings are appropriate to the situation, are exaggerated, or are an overreaction because of my identification with something.

5. I do have influence and power over my feelings.

6. I do not try to own my self as something, to capture self, or to mark self. I understand that such behaviors are only an attempt to kill self as something.

7. I express feelings to let them go.

8. I know it is insane to think that people are controlling how I feel, because I am real and not a product of people's imagination.

9. I know that, even if I have foolishly thought negative thoughts for a while, I can still choose not to take them to heart and so can avoid feeling bad.

10. I know that I can change my negative emotions by acting and thinking in the opposite style or direction from those emotions.

11. I know that I cannot let anyone control my feelings, because no one has control over my mind but me.

12. I know that if I think anxious thoughts long enough, then I will wind up feeling anxious.

13. I know that life cannot control how I feel, because even life cannot control my mind.

14. I know that only I choose to own the things that wind up causing my feelings.

15. I manage my feelings by managing my interpretations and identifying with anything.

16. I only blame myself for how I feel.

17. I only control how I feel, not how others feel.

18. I practice emotional detachment in order to make it a skill that I can use at will.

19. I practice forgiveness for my own peace of mind.

20. I practice forgiveness so I don't have to carry so much.

21. I practice forgiveness so I will be forgiven.

22. I realize that just expressing feelings is not enough.

23. I realize that people can give me the occasion, opportunity, and temptation to feel badly—but only I can choose to feel badly.

24. I see clearly that my feelings are my own.

25. I see that I can choose to take things to heart or not.

26. I see that my stuck or trapped feelings are feelings that I have identified with.

27. I see that when I think a certain way that I then feel that certain way, too.

28. I see the danger of stuck or trapped negative feelings.

29. I seek release from all feelings that are trapped as ideas of self.

30. I seek release from the prison of all ideas of self as self.

31. I take my identity back from my feelings in order to let my feelings flow.

32. I understand that I am not my feelings.

33. I understand that if I don't like the way that I am feeling, then I can change the way that I am behaving and thinking to change how I am feeling.

34. I understand that when I put myself down, I am also putting myself up for putting myself down.

35. I understand that you may want me to feel a certain way, but only I can choose my feelings.

36. If I find that my ventilation of my feelings is just reinforcing or justifying them, then I change my intention to letting go of my feelings.

37. Much of the time, my feelings flow like those of a little child: from moment to moment.

38. Not all feelings are good or healthy, for example, murderous feelings.

39. Since I am not my feelings, I do not have to defend my feelings.

40. Since I am not my feelings, I do not have to hide my feelings.

41. Since I am not my feelings, I do not have to reframe my feelings to make them palatable.

Level 6 Items: Emotional Detachment

On a scale of 1 to 5, how often do you believe the following statements?

1. I am a being, not a doing.

2. I am alive, not something becoming something else.

3. I am detached from all behaviors.

4. I am detached from all experiences.

5. I am detached from all feelings.

6. I am detached from all knowledge.

7. I am detached from all memories.

8. I am detached from all pleasures.

9. I am detached from all sensations.

10. I am free of ideas and thoughts of self.

11. I am not made by my behaviors.

12. I am the container, not the contents.

13. I am that which has my experiences, not my experiences themselves.

14. I am that which has my thoughts, not my thoughts themselves.

15. I believe that no matter how badly my loved ones have hurt and abused me, I must continue to help and support them if I can safely do so.

16. I detach my identity from all of my feelings.

17. I detach my identity from all of my ideas and thoughts of self.

18. I do not accept the opinions of others as to who I am.

19. I do not experience danger to ideas of self, so I am never angry about my ego or self-esteem.

20. I do not get upset when someone blames me for something that they experienced.

21. I do not have any ideas, concepts, or perceptions about my self.

22. I do not have to become something; therefore, I can just flow with life.

23. I do not have to control how you see me in order to control how I feel; therefore, I can just enjoy companionship and life in general.

24. I do not have to control what I am; therefore, I can just be myself.

25. I do not have to defend any ideas of self; therefore, I am never offended.

26. I do not have to protect any ideas of self; therefore, I am never hurt.

27. I do not have to prove that I am anything; therefore, I can just be.

28. I do not have to prove that I am not something; therefore, I can just relax.

29. I do not have to push or promote myself as anything; therefore, I can enjoy and listen to others.

30. I do not have to stop being something; therefore, I have no need to be defensive.

31. I do not seek methods, practices, or systems that give me knowledge to be something or to evolve into something.

32. I do not seek to become something, whether that be behavior, concept, experience, habit, idea, or image.

33. I do not seek to become knowledge about myself.

34. I describe my being, essence, or inner nature when answering the question, "Who am I?"

35. I exist before and after my behaviors.

36. I exist before and after my feelings.

37. I exist before and after my memories.

38. I exist before and after my sensations.

39. I exist before and after my thoughts.

40. I have no concept to be.

41. I have no concept to become.

42. I have no idea who I am—I just have the living experience of being.

43. I have no opinions as to who I am or who I should be.

44. I love even those who dislike or hate me.

45. I love my enemies and pray for them to be under God's will.

46. I understand that those who view themselves as knowledge are the living dead.

47. I use different positive and negative adjectives to describe my behaviors.

48. Nothing can define me.

49. Nothing can limit me as some dead thing.

50. Nothing can trap me as anything.

C6: 8 Basic Emotional Skills

> That which does not kill me, makes me stronger.
>
> —Friedrich Nietzsche

The emotional skills listed below support one another; that is, they are interdependent. However, some of the emotional skills improve and enhance life more than others. Therefore, the skills are listed in their order of relative importance. As a result of this ordering, some skills on the list come before skills that they are dependent upon and cannot exist without.

Many of the skills are context or situation dependent, and many are not. There is some purposeful redundancy. Occasionally, the placement of an ability in one of the eight (8) categories is more arbitrary than not. Feel free to make your own collections based on this list. Use this list to identify your emotional strengths and weakness and then to fortify your emotional strengths and to lessen and overcome your emotional weaknesses.

You can also easily use this list to measure your progress in therapy or in living more maturely. How many of the skills do you practice? How many of the skills are you developing and improving? How many of the skills are you lacking?

Give yourself points for each "yes" answer to the questions for each skill using the following inverse point system: 8 points for each #1 skill; 7 points for each number #2 skill; 6 points for each number #3 skill; 5 points for each number #4 skill; 4 points for each number #5 skill; 3 points for each number #6 skill; 2 points for each number #7 skill; 1 point for each number #8 skill.

Total your score and keep a record of it. Whenever you want to measure your progress, just retake the test and compare it to your old score(s). Higher scores are better, but this test is neither validated nor verified, therefore it cannot be taken too seriously or strictly. Additionally, some skills have more items than other skills, making comparisons between the skills unbalanced or unequal.

Table: 8 Basic Emotional Skills

8 Basic Emotional Skills	
1	Detaching from Feelings
2	Choosing Feelings
3	Directing Feelings
4	Containing Feelings
5	Understanding Feelings
6	Experiencing Feelings
7	Accepting Feelings
8	Sharing Feelings
Copyright © 2017 by Kevin Everett FitzMaurice https://kevinfitzmaurice.com	

Table: Scoring 8 Emotional Skills

Test Results for 8 Basic Emotional Skills			
Skill Tested	**Total Possible**	**Date Tested**	**Score**
1. Detaching	8 x 20 = 160		
2. Choosing	7 x 28 = 196		
3. Directing	6 x 20 = 120		
4. Containing	5 x 20 = 100		
5. Understanding	4 x 26 = 104		
6. Experiencing	3 x 20 = 60		
7. Accepting	2 x 20 = 40		
8. Expressing	1 x 24 = 24		
Total Score	804 points		

1. Detaching, Letting Go, & Freeing Feelings

Detaching from feelings is your ability to free yourself of unwanted feelings. Rather than being the prisoner and victim of a feeling, detaching allows you to free yourself from a feeling so that the feeling might pass. Detaching is your ability to let go of a feeling that you have been hanging on to or have been stuck on.

The detaching skill is needed for most of the other skills to work; therefore, the detaching-feelings skill gets the number one (#1) rating. (For a complete system on how to detach, read FitzMaurice's Garden.)

Here is a list of some of the ways that you can choose to detach from feelings:

1. You can detach your identity from a feeling to let that feeling go. You can also detach your identify from an event to let feelings about that event go.

2. You can detach your ego, pride, or self-esteem from a feeling to let that feeling go. You can also detach your ego, pride, or self-esteem from an event to let feelings about that event go.

3. You can detach your self-story, self-talk, or social-story from a feeling to let that feeling go. You can also detach your self-story or self-talk from an event to let feelings about that event go.

4. You can detach other feelings and feeling memories from a feeling in order to make that feeling less encumbered and so more able to pass.

5. You can detach as many experiences and events from a feeling as you can in order to allow that feeling to dissipate by itself without attachments.

6. You can detach your looping, obsessing, or ruminating from an event to let feelings about that event go.

7. You can detach any need to change or control from an event to let feelings about that event go.

8. You can detach any and all expectations from an event to let feelings about that event go.

9. You can detach any and all desires from an event to let feelings about that event go.

10. You can detach an attitude of importance, intensity, or severity from an event to let feelings about that event go.

11. You can detach extreme or rigid beliefs or interpretations from an event to let feelings about that event go.

12. You can detach any and all claiming (such as claims for abilities or powers) or knowing (such as knowing better or more than others) from an event to let feelings about that event go.

Table: 12 Ways to Detach Feelings

12 Ways to Detach from Feelings	
1	Detach your identity.
2	Detach your ego or self-esteem.
3	Detach your self-story or self-talk.
4	Detach other feelings from it.
5	Detach experiences from it.
6	Detach your looping or obsessing.
7	Detach trying to change or control.
8	Detach all expectations.
9	Detach all desires.
10	Detach all importance.
11	Detach all beliefs & interpretations.
12	Detach all claims & knowing.
More in: *Secret of Maturity, Fourth Edition*	
Copyright © 2017 by Kevin Everett FitzMaurice https://kevinfitzmaurice.com	

To make the most productive use of the strategies from the above table, you should first detach from your feelings about your feelings, for example, your anxiety about your anxiety. Once you detach from an event or feeling, you might choose to reframe, reinterpret, or review the event from one or more new perspectives to generate replacement feelings. However, to remain indifferent or neutral is also an option.

Keys that Support Detachment

Detachment is a skill. Therefore it is helpful to know what key attitudes and feelings promote that skill. Below is a list of some of the key attitudes and feelings to use to develop your skill of detachment.

Practice more of these keys to increase your ability to emotionally detach. Of course, despite these keys naturally making use of and serving detachment, it is also possible to misuse and pervert these keys into serving attachment. The keys are arranged in alphabetical order.

- Acceptance
- Analysis
- Compassion
- Coping
- Creativity

- Flow (absorbed, carried away, or no-mind)
- Forgiveness
- Humor
- Lack of Demands
- Lack of Expectations
- Meditation (providing space)
- Mercy
- Objectivity
- Patiently Following Out
- Perseverance
- Problem Solving
- Rationality
- Relating to Others as Equal
- Relating to Others as the Same
- Relaxation
- Silently Observing
- Silently Witnessing

- Tolerance

- Universality (belief in one human nature)

Attachment Information

Because knowledge is based upon language, and language is based upon words, and words are based upon duality (dualistic definitions such as hot versus cold), it often occurs that one of the best ways to understand something better is to learn to understand its opposite. Here is information to help you better understand the opposite of detachment: attachment.

- Attachment is both necessary and unnecessary depending upon the circumstance, issue, situation, and time.

- Attachment is becoming one, blending, bonding, combining, joining, merging, and uniting with someone or something.

- Identity requires attachment.

- Identification easily leads to attachment.

- Attachment causes feelings, because you take to heart whatever you attach to.

• Repression and suppression require attachment, because you can only repress or suppress something that you are attached to.

• Compulsion and obsession require attachment, because you can only be compulsive or obsessive about something you have attached to.

• Attachment often proves to be self-defeating, because attachment is often the reason that you receive the opposite results from those you consciously desired.

Descriptions for Skill #1

Below are statements that describe the behavior of the person who has the emotional skill of being able to detach from his or her feelings in order to free or release his or her feelings. The statements are not organized in a hierarchical fashion.

1. I am able to detach enough from my feelings to allow myself to think before I react.

2. I am able to detach from my emotions in order to allow myself to plan to take care of my emotions or to plan how to accomplish the desires of my emotions.

3. I am able to laugh at my mistakes and errors, because I am able to detach emotionally from my mistakes and errors.

4. I am aware of myself as the experiencer of feelings, not as the experienced feelings, because I detach from my feelings.

5. I can detach from feelings to just observe feelings whenever I want to or feel the need to.

6. I can let go of any feeling I don't want and let it pass, let it flow, let it be, let it drop, or let it run out by completely detaching from it.

7. I detach from feelings that can be self-destructive (anger, anxiety, depression, guilt, shame) in order to replace them with helpful and effective feelings (concern, disappointment, regret, sadness, sorrow).

8. I do not identify with any of my or other's emotions. I am not my depression, grief, hurt, pain, sorrow, upset, etc. I am not other people's anger, disappointment, guilt, pain, shame, upset, etc.

9. I do not identify with any of the causes of my or others' emotions, because that leads directly to attaching to those feelings.

10. I experience feelings as processes, not as my self, because I am detached from my feelings.

11. I maintain the right relationship between self and feelings: Self is never confused or mingled with feelings.

12. I never have to be a victim of my own feelings, because I can always detach from my feelings and let them rise and fall on their own river of time.

13. I separate myself from my frequent, intense, and chronic emotions in order to let such emotions naturally calm down and subside.

14. I understand the difference between emotions and actions—I see emotions and actions as interrelated but distinct experiences.

15. I detach emotionally from ego and self-esteem judgments in order to objectively and rationally see them for the nonsense that they are.

16. I detach emotionally from self-talk in order to objectively and rationally see if my self-talk is working for me or against me.

17. I detach emotionally from self-stories in order to objectively and rationally see if my self-stories are anything more than just dreams and fantasies.

18. I detach emotionally from my expectations in order to keep my expectations from disturbing me when they are not met.

19. I detach emotionally from my beliefs and interpretations in order to be able to objectively and rationally evaluate the effectiveness and realistic-ness of my beliefs and interpretations.

20. I detach emotionally from my demands and attempts to change and control things in order to avoid the disappointments and frustrations that trying to change or control things often brings.

2. Choosing & Deciding on Feelings

The choosing-of-feelings skill is the key to both emotional responsibility and emotional maturity. Use this skill to regain your personal potency and power. No other skill or method can give you more power over your life; therefore, this skill gets the number two (#2) rating.

Why not the number one (#1) rating? Because you cannot have this skill without the number one skill of detaching. If you cannot detach from a feeling, then you cannot choose to feel differently.

The choosing of feelings is one skill that is composed of four sub-skills.

4 Sub-Skills for Choosing Feelings

The choosing-of-feelings skill is based upon controlling the antecedents and reactions to feelings, not on controlling the feelings themselves. In other words, you control the "before" and "after" of the feeling but not the "what" of the feeling or the feeling itself.

For instance, when you go to a movie, you can choose to keep your expectations low in order to avoid feeling disappointed. You can also control the life expectancy of a feeling or its duration in the "now" of time, but not the "what" or type of the feeling. You control the duration of a feeling by choosing to feed it or not to feed it. You can feed a feeling in at least twelve different ways. (See section "12 Ways to Feed Feelings" below.)

1. You choose your interpretations and responses to an event *before it happens,* because these choices will decide how you will feel about that event. By choosing your intentions, expectations, and interpretations for an event, you have chosen how to feel about that event.

2. You choose your interpretations and responses to a feeling *after you have a feeling,* rather than let your feeling dictate your interpretations and reactions to itself. These choices determine your feelings about your feelings, and your feelings about your feelings either help or hinder your life and goals. In other words, your feelings about your feelings will choose your problem-oriented or solution-oriented responses to your feelings. By choosing your intentions, expectations, and interpretations for a feeling, you have chosen how to feel about that feeling.

3. You choose to feed or to starve a feeling in order to keep the feeling alive or to let the feeling naturally die out. By choosing to feed or starve a feeling, you have chosen to either have that feeling continue or not to have that feeling continue.

4. You know from experience and testing that feelings can either help or hinder your problem-solving and coping. You have learned that some feelings help you in some situations, and other feelings help you in other situations. Therefore, you choose the most productive feelings to suit the situation, and you choose to avoid the most unproductive feelings that do not suit the situation. Through knowing what feelings help or hinder you, you have chosen how to feel by planning what feelings to or not to encourage or elicit in yourself.

5 Things to Control about Feelings

You cannot control a feeling, but you can control the before and after of a feeling and the persistence of a feeling. And if you learn to do those three things well, then you will never feel the need to control a feeling. What you can control is:

1. Whether you will attach your identity to a feeling and keep it stuck or detach your identity from a feeling and let it run its course.

2. Whether you will feed a feeling with attention, connections, thoughts, and time to continue it or starve a feeling from attention, connections, thoughts, and time to let it go.

3. How you will react or respond to a feeling with thoughts, feelings, and actions.

4. How you will feel before something happens by choosing how to interpret and respond to something before it happens.

5. The intensity, frequency, and duration of your feelings by how you cope with, problem-solve, and process your feelings.

Table: 5 Things to Control about Feelings

5 Things to Control about Feelings	
1	Whether to identify with a feeling or not.
2	Whether to feed a feeling or not.
3	How to react or respond to a feeling.
4	How you will feel before an event.
5	How you will fix or cope with a feeling.
More information: *Secret of Maturity, Fourth Edition*	
Copyright © 2017 by Kevin Everett FitzMaurice	https://kevinfitzmaurice.com

12 Ways to Feed Feelings

By understanding how you feed feelings, you can understand how to stop feeding feelings. If people fed positive feelings more than they fed negative feelings, then people would live happier lives. You are in control of what keeps your attention and concern. You are in control of a lot of the stimuli that you let into your life by your choices regarding media, people, places, and things.

This list is mainly the opposite of the previous list on how to detach from feelings.

1. Feed a feeling by making it about you or your identity.

2. Feed a feeling by making it about your ego, pride, or self-esteem.

3. Feed a feeling by making it about your self-story, self-talk, or social-story.

4. Feed a feeling by connecting it to other feelings and feeling memories.

5. Feed a feeling by connecting it to memories of events and experiences.

6. Feed a feeling by thinking about it, and especially in compulsive or repetitious ways.

7. Feed a feeling by trying to change or control it, because that gives it connections, energy, focus, importance, and time.

8. Feed a feeling by having expectations about or for it, because that gives it connections, energy, focus, importance, and time.

9. Feed a feeling by having other feelings about it, and particularly strong desires for or against it.

10. Feed a feeling by considering it dangerous or somehow important and so worthy of your attention, concern, and time.

11. Feed a feeling by having extreme or rigid beliefs or interpretations regarding it.

12. Feed a feeling by claiming abilities or powers for it or by thinking you know a lot about it (pride attachment).

Table: 12 Ways to Feed Feelings

12 Ways to Feed Feelings	
1	Identity with the feeling.
2	Attach your ego or self-esteem.
3	Attach your self-story or self-talk.
4	Attach other feelings to it.
5	Attach experiences to it.
6	Loop on it or obsess about it.
7	Try to change or control or it.
8	Attach expectations to it.
9	Attach desires for or against it.
10	Attach danger or importance to it.
11	Attach beliefs or interpretations to it.
12	Attach claims or knowing to it.
More in: *Secret of Maturity, Fourth Edition*	
Copyright © 2017 by Kevin Everett FitzMaurice https://kevinfitzmaurice.com	

Descriptions for Skill #2

Below are statements that describe the behavior of the person who has the emotional skill of being able to choose his or her feelings. The order of the statements is arbitrary.

1. I am responsible for my feelings, which makes it easy for me to be responsible for my actions.

2. I can discourage any of my self-defeating feelings until they fade away.

3. I can limit, reduce, and even avoid stress reactions. (For example, by limiting my expectations or my judgments that "I know".)

4. I choose not to wallow in self-defeating feelings.

5. I choose to switch feelings in order to bounce back from life's defeats and disappointments.

6. I do not play in emotional manipulation games such as guilt and shame, not even when others insist—insist that I play as I was conditioned to play and have been known to play in the past—by trying to hook me, to push my buttons, or to somehow get me to react and play the game with them.

7. I find my own intentions, expectations, and interpretations to be the major causes of my feelings.

8. I have a high tolerance for frustration that allows me to experiment, fail, go on adventures, make mistakes, take risks, and succeed through failure.

9. I have self-control because my practice of controlling my emotions before and after my emotions happen.

10. I have the necessary thinking and behaving skills to practice emotional regulation.

11. I help and teach others how to deal successfully with their feelings.

12. I keep from any unwanted feeling despite the occasion, opportunity, temptation, or encouragement to have that feeling from my conditioning, my self-talk, or others' conversation or actions.

13. I know the difference between what someone does or says and my emotional reactions to what someone does or says.

14. I never feel helpless about dealing with my feelings.

15. I never have to or want to blame life or others for my feelings.

16. I provide sufficient self-care in the areas of diet, exercise, sleep, support, and social contribution, to alleviate any negative stress from unfulfilled physical or social needs.

17. I recognize the consequences of my emotions on myself, others, and my life; and I take responsibility for those consequences.

18. I refuse responsibility for the feelings of others, but I take responsibility for my impact on the thoughts, feelings, and actions of others.

19. I sometimes choose to act the opposite of the way I feel. This helps me to switch to more helpful thoughts, feelings, and behaviors.

20. I switch behaviors to switch feelings; for instance, I exercise while listening to inspiring or uplifting music when feeling depressed.

21. I switch sensations to switch feelings; for instance, I listen to soothing music when feeling irritated.

22. I switch thoughts to switch feelings; for instance, I think calming and comforting thoughts when feeling anxious.

23. I take responsibility for all of my feelings. I see my choices as the major factor in determining my feelings.

24. I take responsibility for any of my buttons being pushed. No one can insult me without my owning (identifying with) their insult.

25. I take responsibility for the hooks that I throw out, hoping to cause feelings in others or to get others to cause feelings in me.

26. I talk myself out of one feeling and into another feeling whenever I feel the need.

27. I understand the circular cause-and-effect relationship between thinking, feeling, and behaving. And I make use of that understanding to use whichever method (thinking, feeling, behaving) will be the most effective in helping me in the moment to feel in a more healthy way.

28. I understand the interconnected existence and relationship of thinking, feeling, and behaving. And I make use of that understanding to treat thinking, feeling, and behaving as a complete system instead of as three discrete parts.

3. Directing & Using Feelings

Directing feelings is your ability to choose to use your feelings for benefit. Feelings are powerful carriers of energy.

Being able to direct and use the energy of your feelings provides you with many benefits.

You can use feelings to get you motivated and into action. You can use feelings to give you the energy to stand up for what is right or for what you believe. You can use your feelings to give you the force needed to provide protection for the defenseless or weak. Your being able to use your feelings instead of being used by your feelings is important enough to get this skill the number three (#3) rating.

Descriptions for Skill #3

Below are statements that describe the behavior of the person who has the skill of directing and using feelings. This person chooses to use his or her feelings instead of being used by his or her feelings. There is no definite order to the descriptions.

1. I arouse anger in order to defend the defenseless or weak.

2. I arouse compassion in order to assist the needy or helpless.

3. I arouse courage in order to be assertive instead of passive or aggressive.

4. I arouse desire in order to motivate myself to accomplish tasks.

5. I arouse various feelings to help me complete tasks and assignments; for example, I arouse determination and discipline to get some tedious work done.

6. I can assemble my feelings in order to stay absorbed in, concentrated on, and focused on a task.

7. I can collect my energies so that I am in the flow or a creative state.

8. I can delay gratification in order to pursue a goal.

9. I can direct my emotions out of the traps set by those who use guilt or shame to try to dominate, control, manipulate, and negatively motivate me.

10. I can harmonize my emotions with others for the sake of compatibility, belonging, and working as a team.

11. I can keep my feelings directed the way I want them to go, even when others try to redirect my feelings.

12. I can make and keep my word by empowering it with positive emotion.

13. I can redirect compulsive energy from inappropriate tasks to appropriate ones.

14. I direct my energy by directing my feelings.

15. I initialize, start, and engage helpful feelings when I need them.

16. I seek positive experiences and stimuli in order to have positive emotions, and vice versa.

17. I switch from my unwanted feelings to my preferred feelings.

18. I use emotions to connect, relate, and share with others.

19. I use emotions to encourage, inspire, and support others.

20. I use emotions to switch my thinking, feeling, or behaving to more effective and productive forms, depending upon the situation.

4. Protecting, Containing, & Caring for Feelings

Protecting your feelings is your ability to provide an internal safe house to contain your feelings and thereby keep your feelings from contact with internal or external assault, attack, condemnation, suppression, or repression. Often, the best way to protect a feeling is to contain the feeling for another more appropriate audience, place, or time.

Men are often accused of not having feelings when men are really just containing their feelings. The problem for most men is that they don't make time for safely sharing their contained feelings.

This skill is also about your ability to provide care, concern, and nurturance for your own and others' feelings. If you want to connect with others, then learn to care for the feelings of yourself and others through compassion, encouragement, kindness, support, and understanding. If you don't care for your feelings, then you will lose your feelings to darkness (subconsciousness and unconsciousness); therefore, this skill gets the number four (#4) rating.

Descriptions for Skill #4

Below are statements that describe the behavior of the person who has the skill of protecting his or her feelings. The descriptions are not organized in any particular order.

1. I am able to act assertively, because I am able to protect myself from harm when others want to control or change my comments, input, or suggestions.

2. I am aware of my personal areas of emotional vulnerability and weakness and plan to minimize their frequency, intensity, and duration.

3. I am secure in my feelings to the degree of being strong in my emotions.

4. I am tough minded, emotionally tough, and emotionally strong.

5. I build trust in relationships before I expose my deepest layers of feelings.

6. I can contain my feelings so that I can feel them without having to show or share them at the wrong time or place.

7. I can feel one way and act another; for example, I can feel mad without having to act mad.

8. I can tell when it is safe to share my feelings and when it is not.

9. I know how my personal areas of emotional vulnerability can cause me trouble in relationships and activities and plan accordingly.

10. I make a safe time and place for my feelings.

11. I make sure to take care of the self-care basics: diet, sleep, exercise, support, sharing, and social contribution.

12. I protect any of my vulnerable feelings from attack or abuse if and when they are exposed to attack or abuse.

13. I protect my personal areas of emotional vulnerability from abusive or exploitive exposure.

14. I soothe my own hurt feelings by taking care of my own needs and wants.

15. I take care of myself when I am under a lot of stress; for example, I make sure to provide some time alone, some time for spirituality, and some time to relax.

16. I tolerate silence in conversation and allow space for feelings.

17. I value openness in relationships and develop trust to allow emotional openness to safely occur.

18. I protect my feelings by practicing my emotional coping skills.

19. I create environments that are protective and conducive to allowing me to experience my negative feelings such as having a meditation place and time for them.

20. I know the right people to share my negative feelings with who will both honor those feelings and help me to let them go.

5. Understanding Feelings: Emotional Insight

Understanding feelings is your ability to understand—physically, tonally, and verbally—the feelings you or others are trying to or not to express. For example, in the phony, ritualistic, and political world of adult relationships, it is important to be able to read the emotional intentions of others. If you do not have the insight that you are feeling hurt and so angry, then you will not take appropriate action to care for yourself and to alleviate those feelings.

To have insight into your and others' emotional states will help you to avoid many communication pitfalls and social blunders. For example, if you can see that someone is upset, then you can refrain from sharing the joke that you had planned to share and, instead, respond in a more empathic way. Emotional insight is the key to being able to motivate yourself to switch from unwanted thoughts, feelings, and behaviors to wanted thoughts, feelings, and behaviors; therefore, emotional insight gets the number five (#5) rating. After all, how can you switch feelings if you don't first see a need?

Descriptions for Skill #5

Below are statements that describe the behavior of the person who has the skill of understanding their own and others' feelings. The descriptions are not listed in a particular order.

1. I accurately reflect to others what they are feeling.

2. I am sensitive to the implied versus the expressed feelings of others.

3. I can easily listen to others, because I appreciate their emotional communication over their verbal communication.

4. I can figure out and plan how to respond to complex interpersonal situations by understanding the emotions that are driving each person's behaviors.

5. I can figure out and understand relationships through understanding the emotional intentions, expectations, interpretations, and needs of the persons concerned.

6. I can negotiate and resolve interpersonal conflicts through understanding the emotional intentions, expectations, interpretations, needs, and concerns of both or all sides.

7. I can tell which feelings I can trust to guide me by their clarity and depth.

8. I can trace any one of my feelings to its root causes.

9. I can understand others' emotional points of view and perspectives.

10. I empathize with others—that is, I can feel the feelings of others.

11. I have a high emotional intelligence quotient (IQ) that I regard as more practical, useful, and significant than the language or math IQ I got in school.

12. I hear and understand the emotional message over the verbal message of my own communications, as well as others' communications.

13. I hear the feeling behind the feeling; for instance, I sense the hurt behind anger.

14. I know how and when to lead—and how and when to follow—by the emotions in the group and myself.

15. I know how to solve problems in relationships by solving how the people involved interpret each other's emotions.

16. I know when I am being ruled by rules (TA's parent ego state), reason (TA's adult ego state), or emotion (TA's child ego state).

17. I note emotional habits and patterns in myself and others.

18. I observe conflicting signals between what people are saying verbally, tonally, and physically.

19. I observe the prime directive in people to be the intentions of their feelings; that is, I see how people are motivated by feelings over all else, including reason, logic, rules, ideals, and conditioning.

20. I rely more on people's physical and tonal emotional cues than people's verbal signals.

21. I understand emotional intentions, expectations, interpretations, needs, desires, purposes, and goals.

22. I understand the emotional messages in body language and physical contact.

23. I understand the emotional messages in voice tone and pitch including such differences as inflections and intonations.

24. I understand the emotional needs of others and live by the golden rule of not attempting to inflict on others what I wouldn't want inflicted on me; for example, I do not use put-downs as a way to try to control or motivate the behavior of others.

25. I understand the need for cooperation, sharing, and caring in order to allow emotional beings to work well together.

26. I use the win-win model of negotiation by understanding and accounting for the emotional intentions, expectations, interpretations, and needs of all parties concerned.

6. Allowing & Experiencing Feelings

Allowing feelings is your permitting your feelings full internal expression. While you might accept the fact of a feeling, you might still deny its full expression. With the allowing-feelings skill, you can experience the full range of any feeling or matrix of feelings.

By now, you should be able to see how interdependent all of the emotional skills are. For instance, how could you have some of the above skills if you did not allow yourself to experience your feelings? The allowing feeling skill is necessary for you to be "true to yourself," to admit to yourself what you really feel; therefore, the allowing-feeling skill gets the number six (#6) rating.

Descriptions for Skill #6

Below are statements that describe the behavior of the person who has the skill of allowing his or her feelings full internal expression. There is no definite order to this listing of the descriptions.

1. I admit and take responsibility for emotions that are mostly or always unhealthy and harmful, such as rage, hate, envy, greed, gluttony, sloth, lust, sadistic pleasure, and pride. I work diligently to release, eliminate, and prevent unhealthy and harmful feelings.

2. I allow all of my feelings full natural inner or outer expression as the situation warrants.

3. I allow feelings to be the nonverbal energy patterns that they are.

4. I allow my heart to make contact with and have feeling experiences with many things.

5. I can allow myself to experience being alone without having to feel lonely.

6. I can sit with a feeling without having to name, analyze, or influence it.

7. I experience conflicting emotions without having to control the conflict.

8. I experience feelings without any desire to capture, control, correct, criticize, condemn, change, or cover them.

9. I experience feelings without being afraid to experience them; for instance, I find grief allows me to process my responses so as to move on over time.

10. I experience love without worrying about anything else—for example, worrying about my vulnerability or identity in that love.

11. I experience my feelings as sensations of sensations or sensations of experiences.

12. I find both humility and gratitude from feeling sad for sensible periods of time.

13. I re-experience my suppressed and repressed feelings.

14. I recognize the determination to do better that I get from realistic depression.

15. I recognize the difference between having a feeling and acting on a feeling; for example, I can feel angry about environmental problems and work positively to end them.

16. I recognize the motivation to plan and prepare that I get from practical anxiety.

17. I recognize the motivational power of anger to right wrongs.

18. I recognize the need to better hold to my own ideals that I get from constructive guilt.

19. I recognize the social learning that I get from constructive shame.

20. I switch from one strong feeling to another without hesitation or reservation, as freely as does a little child.

7. Accepting Recognized or Identified Feelings

> Wherefore by their fruits ye shall know them.
>
> —Matthew 7:20

Accepting feelings is your ability to accept the fact of a feeling rather than to deny the existence of a feeling for any reason.

Acceptance is not condoning. Yes, there are good and bad feelings just as there are good and bad thoughts or actions. You can tell the difference between good and bad feelings by their positive or negative results. Albert Ellis, the founder of REBT, published a contrasting list of healthy versus unhealthy feelings that is available in the REBT literature. For instance, Ellis taught that frustration is preferred over depression, sorrow is preferred over despair, and sadness is preferred over shame. Feelings can also be contrasted as helpful versus unhelpful for your happiness and intentions. A list of healthy versus unhealthy feelings can be found in *Planet Earth: Insane Asylum for the Universe, Second Edition* and in *Journal Journey from Ego*.

Recognizing, labeling, and identifying feelings is an important skill in popular psychology. However, in creative and joyful living, the ability to experience your feelings without labeling your feelings is a higher skill. The naming of a feeling will either break your contact with that feeling or distance you from that feeling so that your experience of that feeling is either ended or diminished. This book does not consider the labeling of feelings to be an emotional skill; however, the naming of feelings could be considered a mental or thinking skill.

Without acceptance of feelings, there is no choosing of good feelings over bad. Without the acceptance of feelings, the other emotional skills cannot exist. You need to accept "what is" before you can act on "what is"; therefore, the accepting-of-feelings skill gets the number seven (#7) rating.

Descriptions for Skill #7

Below are statements that describe the behavior of the person who has the skill of accepting the feelings of himself or herself and of others. The order of the descriptions is unorganized.

1. I accept all feelings, but I do not approve of all feelings.

2. I accept and allow any feeling that I have.

3. I accept my feelings as they are occurring—that is, I accept my feelings in the here and now.

4. I accept my feelings even when I have more than one feeling about something.

5. I accept that my feelings control my choices; therefore, I accept my feelings before, during, and after my choices.

6. I accept the frequency of my emotions.

7. I allow feelings to just be what they are, without having to categorize or label them.

8. I allow my feelings to continue until they are done.

9. I allow the intensity of my and others' feelings and emotions.

10. I avoid distancing myself from my feelings by labeling my feelings.

11. I avoid escaping my feelings by labeling my feelings.

12. I avoid needing to damn or deify my feelings as methods of escaping from or of controlling my feelings.

13. I can accept any feeling that I am aware of in myself or others.

14. I can allow my feelings to run their natural course.

15. I choose not to suppress or repress my feelings, but instead, to develop the skills needed to process and deal with my feelings.

16. I just accept my feelings for what they are: energy patterns and waves.

17. I just accept my feelings for what they are: energy reactions to sensations.

18. I just accept my feelings for what they are: sensations of sensations.

19. I never feel the need to depend on rationalizations, excuses, or justifications for my feelings.

20. I understand that naming can be useful for remembering and organizing, but I also know that naming ends experiencing whether it is the enjoyment of a sunset or the eating of an ice-cream cone.

8. Expressing & Sharing Feelings

Expressing feelings is your ability to physically, tonally, and verbally express feelings so that others understand what you are feeling. It is also the skill area for being able to share your understanding of others' feelings with them. While many sincere therapists believe this skill holds the key to therapy, this is the least important emotional skill. This is an important skill, but one that rarely deserves the credit that is often given to it—credit that should, instead, go to one or more of the other emotional skills.

Most likely, the confusion surrounding this skill results from the previous lack of differentiation of the emotional skills and the assumption or misconception that this skill contains some of or all of the other emotional skills. When therapists get clients to use this skill, the main ensuing benefits come not from this skill but, rather, from the emotional skills needed in order to use this skill. For example, expressing grief requires the emotional skills of at least accepting and allowing your feelings of grief. Expressing might well involve other emotional skills, as well—for instance, protecting or containing the emotion in need of expression.

Hopefully, expressing feelings will lead to the skills of detaching and choosing, as they are the two primary life changing and life improving emotional skills that we all need more of. Since none of the other emotional skills are dependent upon the skill of expressing feelings, though many of them make use of it, this skill comes in last place: number eight (#8).

Descriptions for Skill #8

Below are statements that describe the behavior of the person who has the skill of effectively expressing and communicating their feelings. This list is numbered but not ordered.

1. I am a better communicator due to my ability to express what I am feeling.

2. I am emotionally expressive.

3. I ask open-ended questions in order to help people explore their feelings.

4. I attend to feelings in myself and others without having to intellectualize about them.

5. I can effectively paraphrase and summarize my and others' feelings.

6. I can express my anger assertively rather than aggressively, passively, or passive-aggressively.

7. I can express my emotions internally or externally.

8. I can let people know what I feel and want without blaming them for how I feel.

9. I communicate feelings accurately, both inside my self and to others.

10. I describe emotions accurately, both for my own sake and for the sake of others.

11. I encourage others to keep talking about their feelings with my empathy, acceptance, and genuineness.

12. I express—ventilate—some of my feelings as a means of releasing them, of letting them go, not as a means of reinforcing them.

13. I first talk about myself when talking about my feelings; that is, I avoid blaming others by making use of "I" messages.

14. I get others to open up about their feelings.

15. I help people accept their feelings.

16. I help people clarify what they are feeling.

17. I help people to take responsibility for their feelings.

18. I share my feelings with others and feel emotionally understood.

19. I use emotions to effectively communicate.

20. I use emotions to effectively influence myself and others.

21. I use emotions to effectively motivate myself and others.

22. I validate my own and other people's feelings.

23. In an emotional fight, I choose to fight fair by refusing to attack the personhood or identity of the other person.

24. I can share my negative feelings with others as a way to discount and minimize those feelings in myself and others by exposing those negative feelings for the foolishness that they are and tend to result in.

Table: Scoring 8 Emotional Skills

Test Results for 8 Basic Emotional Skills			
Skill Tested	Total Possible	Date Tested	Score
1. Detaching	8 x 20 = 160		
2. Choosing	7 x 28 = 196		
3. Directing	6 x 20 = 120		
4. Containing	5 x 20 = 100		
5. Understanding	4 x 26 = 104		
6. Experiencing	3 x 20 = 60		
7. Accepting	2 x 20 = 40		
8. Expressing	1 x 24 = 24		
Total Score	804 points		

C7: STPHFR Paradigm of Feeling Causation

3 Stages of Understanding Causation

> Between stimulus and response, there is a space. In that space is our power to choose our response. In our response lies our growth and our freedom.
>
> — Viktor Frankl, *Man's Search for Meaning*

Definitions of Terms

• A paradigm is a diagram, map, model, or pattern for understanding an area of inquiry or research.

A paradigm is an approach to something; therefore, a paradigm helps you to see and understand something but only according to its assumptions. A paradigm can help you to see or blind you to seeing what the paradigm is not looking for.

• A stimulus (S) is any event or action that elicits or causes a response.

A stimulus can also be defined as anything that you consciously notice or that you pay attention to. Whatever gets your attention can be considered to be a stimulus.

• A response (R) is any action or reaction in regard to a stimulus.

When you react to something that happens, then what happened is the stimulus (S) and how you reacted to it is your response (R) to that stimulus.

• The word hearting (H) means: taking to heart or to touch with your life force. Hearting is sensing with your heart.

Hearting can be mistaken for identifying the self with something, because when you identify your self with something there is an almost irresistible tendency to take that identification or identity to heart.

Hearting as a process is indicated by the following words or phrases: attached, being entangled, being hooked, being overly sensitive, being owned, being sensitive, believing deeply, coming directly in contact with, emotionally weak, emotionally vulnerable, enmeshed, feeling deeply, in touch with, owning something, take to heart, taking something too seriously, they got to you, too attached, wearing your heart on your sleeve, you let them get to you.

• STPHFR or S-T-P-H-F-R is an acronym that is pronounced just like the word "stiffer". STPHFR stands for Stimulus, Thinking, Playback, Hearting, Feeling, Response.

Stage 1: Stimulus-Response (S-R)

> One should not wrongly reify 'cause' and 'effect,' as the natural scientists do (and whoever, like them, now 'naturalizes' in his thinking), according to the prevailing mechanical doltishness which makes the cause press and push until it 'effects' its end; one should use 'cause' and 'effect' only as pure concepts, that is to say, as

> conventional fictions for the purpose of designation and communication—not for explanation.
>
> —Friedrich Nietzsche

• Science is based upon the stimulus-response (S-R) paradigm.

• Scientists note some effect, some response (R), and ask: Why that response? What stimulus (S) caused that response (R)?

• Scientists note some stimulus (S) and try to predict the response (R) that will follow from that stimulus (S).

• Scientists have a response (R) that they want, and try to determine the stimulus (S) that they will need to gain that response (R).

• Scientists use the scientific method to verify and prove S-R connections and responses as being rules or regular outcomes. It is only by repeated testing and reliable results from such testing that scientists should say anything about anything. Whatever the scientific method of verification cannot be applied to is not currently part of the domain of science.

> One can sum up all this by saying that the criterion of the scientific status of a

> theory is its falsifiability, or refutability, or testability.
>
> —Karl Popper

The accurate prediction of stimulus-response (S-R) relations has led to the development of modern technology. We have been able to place a man on the moon, because we understand how to accurately determine S-R connections, patterns, and relationships.

Excited by the effectiveness of the stimulus-response (S-R) paradigm, people began to use the S-R paradigm to help them to understand human behavior and motivation. A new field of psychology grew up with the strongest adherents and developments occurring in the United States. This new field was named Behaviorism.

Despite all the promise of Behaviorism and the wealth of information gained from its research projects, Behaviorism fell far short of understanding and predicting human behavior and motivation. In order to survive, Behaviorism eventually narrowed its scope to manipulating human behavior through adding reinforcements or the denial and removal of reinforcements (behavioral rewards).

Behaviorism has contributed greatly to human understanding of: behavior change by controlling rewards, conditioned responses, conditioning, learned behavior, motivation through reward, and the un-conditioning and reconditioning of conditioned responses.

Behaviorism has had some success understanding human motivation, but so little that few psychologists today rely exclusively on Behaviorism. The less one thinks, the more applicable Behaviorism is; hence, young children and the mentally handicapped continue to receive the most programs and interventions based upon Behaviorism.

In summary, the S-R paradigm is excellent for dead or nonliving things but of much less practical value for understanding and predicting the behavior of living beings–particularly human beings who think and those who think about their thinking.

Stage 2: S-T-R Paradigm

Cognitive psychotherapies propose the problem with Behaviorism is that the S-R paradigm is not relevant for intelligent living beings. Intelligent living beings are those who think to plan their responses before a stimulus occurs, those who think to choose a response to an occurring stimulus, and those who analyze their responses to stimuli after they happen.

The most comprehensive cognitive psychotherapy, Rational Emotive Behavior Therapy (REBT), suggests a stimulus-thinking-response (S-T-R) paradigm for understanding human beings. (For more information, see "Table: REBT's ABCs of Emotions" in chapter *C8: Assorted Additions*.)

It is reasoned that—in-between the stimulus (S) received by a living being and its response (R) to that stimulus (S)–there is the mental or instinctual processing (T) of that stimulus, either consciously or unconsciously.

REBT asserts that for living beings, the thinking (T) part controls the response (R) part far more than does the stimulus (S) part. The thinking part might be unconscious conditioning, automatic habit, or conscious thinking and choosing.

In other words, your thinking (T) affects your response (R) far more than what happens (S) to you affects your response (R). For example, if an animal has an instinctual response to flee or fly away from sudden loud noises (T), then even if a sudden loud noise (S) is not a threat and so no cause to flee, the animal will still flee or fly away (R). (Yes, behavioral conditioning can often be used to mitigate and even overcome such instinctual responses (T) over time or vice versa.)

• This S-T-R model can be further simplified into sayings such as:

"If you think angry thoughts you will become angry."

"Change your thinking and change your feeling."

"If you think anxious thoughts, you will become anxious even if there is nothing (no outside stimulus, S) to get anxious about."

Stage 3: STPHFR Paradigm

While the S-T-R paradigm is a significant development beyond the oversimplified S-R paradigm, the S-T-R model does not adequately account for human emotions and motivations.

- There is more going on between S and R than just plain or simple thinking.

If your feelings were simply the result of what you thought, then whenever you had negative thoughts, you would also have negative feelings. However, it simply is not true that you feel all of your thoughts. Additionally, it is also not true that all of your feelings come from your thoughts.

- We need a more comprehensive model than the S-T-R paradigm.

The real cause for feelings is contact with the inner energy that is in the heart, the seat for the life force. When the life force, your life energy, contacts (H) any thing–you will have feelings (F) about whatever was contacted. The heart can make contact with anything that you sense in your internal world, with anything that you sense in your body, and with anything that you sense in your external world.

What the heart makes contact with in all cases is sensations or the results of other sensing processes (soul, mind, body). The heart makes contact by sensing some preexisting sensations with energy, feeling with them energy, or touching them with energy. To oversimplify, the sensations contacted by the heart can be sensations of things, thoughts, or feelings.

Your life force can feel (touch) sensations from your outer senses (your body's senses), or your life force can feel (touch) sensations from your inner senses (soul or mind senses). For example, when the pleasing sensations from having a body massage are taken to heart–they produce positive feelings. For example, when the negative sensations from negative thoughts are taken to heart–they produce negative feelings.

Your heart can have feelings by touching your thoughts, images, or memories. You can even have feelings of feelings. Your heart can have feelings by touching sensations of: your body, your imaginary self (ego, self-esteem), your mind, your physical environment, your real self, your soul, and your spiritual environment.

Some observations based upon the STPHFR paradigm follow:

- Feelings are sensations of whatever was felt or touched by the heart, including any other sensations or feelings that were touched.

- Feelings (F) are sensations that are produced, energized, and amplified by the life force coming into contact (H) with the sensing of some inner, bodily, or outer event.

• Feelings are sensations of sensations, not thoughts (T).

• Sensations "cause" feelings (F), not thoughts (T).

• Only thoughts that you have sensations of can be felt by the heart and thereby result in feelings.

• Your heart does not have to contact what you sense in your internal world, in your body, or your external world.

• Hearting is a choice, but conditioning, habit, and unconscious responses can make hearting automatic.

• You cannot take something to heart, sense something with your heart, and not have feelings about it.

• Identifying with something will more than likely result in your taking that thing to heart. Identity is too personal and important for the heart not to want to know it by sensing it, by contacting it.

• Feelings direct behaviors (R), not thoughts (T).

• Sensations are life, not thoughts or images (T).

STPHFR As Emotional Responsibility

• S-T-P-H-F-R: Stimulus-Thinking-Playback-Hearting-Feeling-Response.

• Note the number of choice points (5) in-between the stimulus (S) and the response (R). There is a choice point after S, T, P, H, and F.

Generic or Basic STPHFR Model

S = What happened? What event or experience am I responding to?

T = What am I thinking about the stimulus (S) that got my attention?

P = What thoughts (T) am I playing back over and over again in my mind about S?

H = What thoughts (T) did I buy into, identify with, own, or take to heart?

F = What feelings am I having about what I owned (H)?

R = What is my response to (S) based upon my feelings (F) about (H)?

STPHFR Model of Emotions & Behaviors

One of the important insights needed to understand and deal effectively with feelings is to understand what it was that was: contacted, felt by your life force, owned, sensed, swallowed, taken to heart, or touched by your heart.

- To know why you feel the way that you do–find out what you took to heart.

Your feelings (F) are part of your reactions to events (S). Feelings (F) are reactions that produce behavioral responses (R). The results from the science of selling show that even when people think they are buying something because of their research, practical considerations, or logical deductions, people are still buying based upon how they feel about something. (For a book on selling that is based on over 1,000 scientific research studies, read *The Science of Selling* by David Hoffeld.)

- Emotion causes motion.

All behaviors are motivated by feelings. All actions require energy and feelings are the energy that drives the actions of the living. Your response (R) is your behavioral reaction. Behavioral responses (R) are dependent upon feeling (F) reactions. Feelings are based on contacting sensations. Sensations are based upon paying attention to something. You are responsible for what you pay attention to and what you take to heart; therefore, you are responsible for how you feel.

• Feelings are one of three kinds: negative, neutral, or positive.

If you want to influence, control, or change a problem—it makes sense to concentrate on what you have the most control over that will produce the greatest change. Because of this logic, this book teaches you to work at controlling (1) what you think, (2) what thoughts you repeat, and (3) what you take to heart.

While you can sometimes control the stimulus (S) itself, more often you cannot. However, you always have control over what you think (T), what thoughts you playback (P) or continue to think, and what you take to heart (H) unless you are brain damaged, psychotic, or in a coma.

• You must decide what to think, what thoughts to playback, and what to take to heart. No one can do that for you.

Yes, you have some bad thinking, repeating, and hearting habits that are on autopilot (subconscious or unconscious). But you can make these subconscious and unconscious habits, programs, or scripts conscious again. They were, after all, conscious before you conditioned or programmed them to the point that they became habits. Yes, others taught you bad habits. But others cannot change your habits for you.

Yes, you should still try to affect the stimulus (S) when reasonably possible. However, your greatest energy should be applied where you will have the greatest effect and benefit: on controlling what you choose to think (T), what thoughts you choose to playback (P), and what you contact (H) with your inner energy.

If you want to change or control a feeling (F), which is a reaction to a sensation, then you need to change or control what happens before or after the feeling arises.

The surest way to control a feeling is to control what you take to heart (H). If you do not take something to heart (H), you cannot have feelings about it.

The surest way to control what you take to heart (H) is to control what you playback (P)–because you only take to heart (H) what you playback (P). Playback includes identifying with something, making something about your ego or self-esteem, adding feelings and experiences to new experiences (S), obsessing about (S), trying to change or control (S), having expectations or desires about (S), making (S) important or dangerous, and having beliefs or interpretations about (S).

Another way to understand the issue of what is affecting you is to realize that you cannot be affected by anything but your mind. All external events are interpreted and represented by your mind only after they have passed.

• The only real stimulus (S) for you is your mind, your thinking (T) and (P).

Your reaction to your thinking about an event is either to playback (P) your thinking and so to take your thinking to heart (H), or not to playback your thinking and to just let the event go, let it be, let it pass.

While this is an obvious oversimplification, because not all sensations come from thinking (T) or (P), it is an easy place for you to begin to regain your personal power: emotional responsibility as the key to your mental health.

Developing the insight and emotional skills needed to control what you take to heart and what you do not take to heart is the first step in learning to apply emotional maturity no matter what your particular counseling issue is when you first come into counseling. Emotional skills are needed for therapy to be effective. Leave any counseling or therapy that does not actively teach at least both emotional and coping skills. Let the charlatans and magicians work on someone else.

Responsibility is the key to a mature life. You already know about behavioral responsibility. Now it is time for you to learn and to practice mental and emotional responsibility.

Unless you have a more serious condition than can be treated in an outpatient counseling setting, it is time for you to say, "Only I made me think that," "Only I made me dwell on that," and "Only I made me feel that way."

Yes, others can create the occasion, the opportunity, the temptation, and the stimulus that you think about, repeat, and that you take sensations to heart about. But others cannot choose your thoughts (T) or what thoughts you repeat, playback (P). And others cannot choose to take your sensations of the stimulus or your thoughts to heart (H). True, as a child others seemed to have and to exercise power over your thoughts and feelings, but now, as an adult, you can choose to see through those games and manipulations.

Only you are responsible for your choices and isn't that wonderful! Else what would you be!? Not a human being, but a mere robot, a puppet, a figment of someone's imagination, or a zombie.

Time to grow up, to become mature, and to become responsible for all of you: emotional, mental, and behavioral. Then you will be ready for the final phase of maturity: spiritual responsibility.

Table: STPHFR 6 Steps

Use this table for a fast and effective reminder of the STPHFR model.

STPHFR: 6 Steps of Feeling & Behaving	
S =	What event, experience, or memory got your attention?
T =	What are you thinking about the stimulus (S)?
P =	What thoughts (T) are you playing back over again about S?
H =	What (T) did you buy into, identify with, own, or take to heart?
F =	What feelings are you having about what you owned (H)?
R =	What is your response to your feelings (F) about (H)?
Copyright © 2017 by Kevin Everett FitzMaurice	https://kevinfitzmaurice.com

STPHFR Infographic

The below infographic on STPHR can be read more easily at: https://kevinfitzmaurice.com/free-stuff/responsibility-issues/stphfr-infographic/.

On the author's website, this infographic is in color and the Portable Network Graphics (PNG) format. The PNG format allows the sizing of the image while retaining the full quality or resolution of the image. PNG is particularly useful for mobile devices.

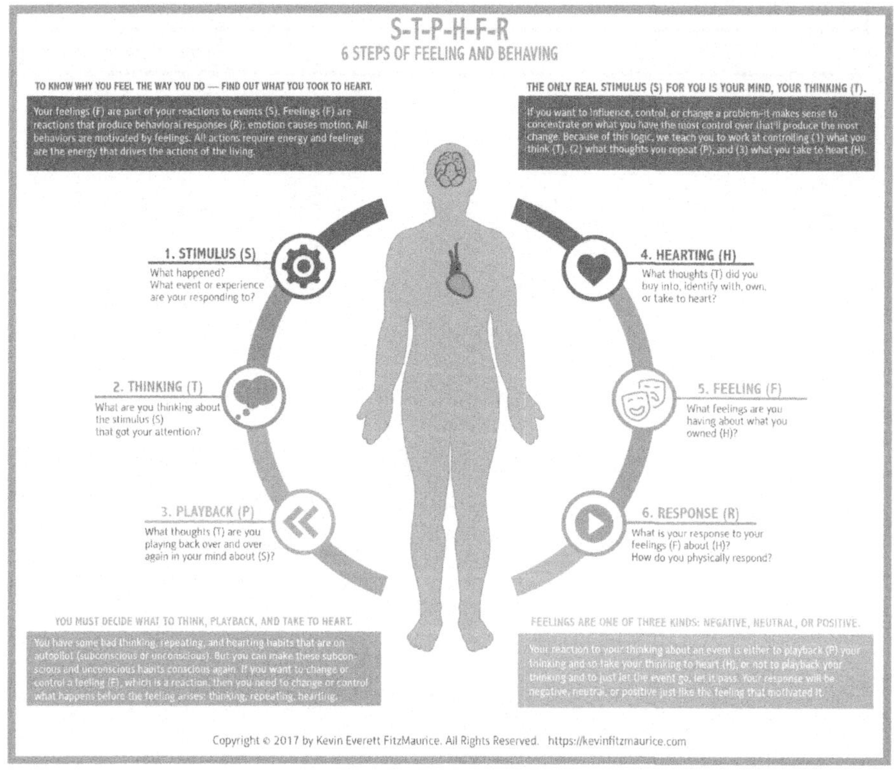

STPHFR Insights

This section is a list of thoughts about the nature of experience based upon the STPHFR paradigm. It requires a full understanding of the STPHFR model. But this section is not necessary for the application or daily use of the STPHFR paradigm. You can ignore this section and come back to it later when you are more experienced and practiced using the STPHFR paradigm.

STPHFR: S = Stimulus, T = Thinking, P = Playback, H = Hearting, F = Feeling, R = Response.

For the sake of the observations below, P is often referred to as T or grouped with T, because P is only a type of T. An understanding of General Semantics would make this section easier to process. Consider reading We're All Insane! Second Edition as an aid to understanding this section.

1. S exists but not for T.

2. S exists independently of T or F.

3. S for me is about H's contact with S.

4. F is about H's contact.

5. F can be about H's contact with T or S.

6. F about T can never be about S.

7. F derived directly from S is about S.

8. F is mainly about F, not S or even T.

9. F cannot be about T and S at the same time.

10. T can be about F, not S.

11. I can only be aware of S by F.

12. I can be aware of T by T or F.

13. I can be aware of F by T or F.

14. I can be aware of T as T or F, but it is only T.

15. I can be aware of F as F or T, but is is only F.

16. I cannot be aware of S except as F.

17. I readily confuse H's contact with T with H's contact with S.

18. I readily confuse T with S.

19. I readily confuse T with F.

20. H + T = F

21. H + S = F

22. H + T + S = F2

23. T = F – H

24. S = F – H

25. S does not = T

26. S does not = R

27. F does equal a part of S if it comes from H + S.

28. S can be experienced in part through F but never known even in part with T.

29. F can be both experienced and known in part through T.

30. R is really caused by H.

31. Control P and H and let S, T, and F be free.

32. P is recursive T.

• Since all that I can respond to is my mind, is T or F–I will focus first on making my mind right, not S.

• It's all in my mind, in T or F–because there is no place else it can be for me.

C8: Assorted Additions

What you believe you experience.

—J. Krishnamurti

3 Scales for Maturity

The three scales presented start with simple duality or two perspectives, move to triality or three perspectives, and wind up with an advanced system of five simultaneous perspectives. (For more information and an in-depth analysis of triality, read *World Within: The Inner Life*.)

Dualistic Scale for Maturity

This scale is based on duality or opposites. One column shows a negative immature characteristic and the opposing column shows a positive mature characteristic. There are a total of six tables to cover the one hundred and twenty-seven (127) characteristics or items on the scale.

Technically, this first scale is not a scale since it only has two points. However, it is being characterized a scale for comparison with the other two scales that follow.

Number	IMMATURE	MATURE
1	unaccountable, irresponsible	responsible, accountable
2	undependable, unreliable	reliable, honorable, dependable
3	undeveloped	mellow, judicious
4	supported by environment	self-supported, self-contained
5	environmentally dependent	self-reliant, self-sufficient
6	having external locus of control	having internal locus of control, self-ruled
7	outer-directed	inner-directed, having self-determination
8	externally responsible	internally responsible
9	controlled, dependent	self-directing, self-restrained
10	being a loser or follower	self-governed, self-conquering
11	helpless, weak, dependent	self-directing, having autonomy
12	willful, contrary	self-controlling, self-denial, self-sacrificing
13	hedonistic, uncivilized	self-disciplined, self-mastering
14	constrained, nonassertive	assertive, outspoken
15	conditioned, programmed	free, unbound, spontaneous
16	muffled, suffocated, smothered	unique, inimitable
17	lost, undifferentiated	differentiated, distinguished
18	having unclear domains	having clear domains
19	having unclear boundaries	having clear (demarcated) boundaries
20	unclear, tight, closed	open, spacious, clear

Number	IMMATURE	MATURE
21	stagnating, dead	growing, magnifying, moving
22	non-mutual, pseudo-mutual	mutual, giving *quid pro quo*
23	leeching, symbiotic	mutual, reciprocal, complementary
24	parasitic, symbiotic	together, joint, associated
25	other-directed, codependent	inner-directed, independent, freethinking
26	macho, cutie, phony	real, sincere, earnest
27	changing, guileful, pseudo-self	true to self, sound, stable
28	unreal, fake, unauthentic	authentic, genuine, real
29	inconsistent, incongruent	congruent, consistent, concerted
30	mindless, being a follower	individualistic, having integrity, having wholeness
31	disharmonious, unintegrated	integrated, flowing, concordant
32	libertine, being a dissipater	chaste, innocent, pure, wholesome
33	unfocused, uncentered	centered, focused, living in the internal marrow
34	mechanical, uncaring	empathic, feeling
35	unresponsive, insensitive	sensitive, responsive
36	self-indulgent, emotionally dependent	emotionally independent
37	playing the Blame Game, practicing disownership of feelings	practicing ownership of feelings
38	perturbed, easily upset	stoic, composed, equanimous
39	looking to others, being a product of others	self-ownership, self-assured
40	unwilling to suffer short-term pain	willing suffer short-term pain

Number	IMMATURE	MATURE
41	pretentious, snobbish, being a braggart	retiring, demure, unobtrusive
42	self-defeating, excusing, blaming	admitting error
43	paralogizing, rationalizing	admitting fault, game-free
44	non-discriminating, chosen for	choosing, discriminating
45	intolerant, accepting	accepting, resigned
46	echoing, blind following	testing, investigating, searching
47	swallowing, believing that you have no options	challenging, questioning, disputing
48	manipulated, reactive, having a push button	proactive, volition
49	rebounding, reacting	choosing, selective
50	onlooking, spectating, observing	participating
51	broken, crooked, dishonest	honest, straight, serene, whole
52	self-suppressing	self-discovering
53	having knowledge of others	having self-knowledge
54	dark, unconscious	conscious, light
55	dead, asleep, unaware	aware, awake, alive
56	blind, knowing	perceptive, insightful
57	putting up a front, wearing masks, hiding behind a role	practicing self-disclosure
58	stuffing, conforming	self-expressing
59	discounting	nurturing, encouraging, supportive
60	disqualifying, disconfirming	confirming, fostering

Number	IMMATURE	MATURE
61	fragmented, in pieces, unintegrated	integrated, unified, harmonious
62	practicing simple cause-and-effect thinking	practicing systemic thinking
63	practicing linear thinking	ecological, practicing cybernetic thinking
64	closed-minded	open-minded, broad-minded
65	illogical, irrational	rational, logical
66	foolish, having book knowledge	sensible, having common sense
67	prejudiced, subjective	objective, unprejudiced
68	practicing group or peer pressure	practicing independent thought
69	one-dimensional, pedantic	creative, inspired
70	opinionated, being a know-it-all	wise, discerning
71	practicing negative thinking	practicing positive thinking
72	cynical, pessimistic	optimistic, idealistic, being a visionary
73	anxious, distressed, worried	hopeful, assured, confident
74	unquiet, uneasy, impatient	patient, having sangfroid, having aplomb
75	intolerant, being a small person	tolerant, being a big person
76	fixed, rigid	open to change
77	hostile, lustful, hateful	loving, warm, intimate, gregarious
78	dull, boring, common	vital, full of life
79	hating others as self	loving others as self
80	resentful, grudging	forgiving, merciful

Number	IMMATURE	MATURE
81	fragmented, in pieces, unintegrated	integrated, unified, harmonious
82	practicing simple cause-and-effect thinking	practicing systemic thinking
83	practicing linear thinking	ecological, practicing cybernetic thinking
84	closed-minded	open-minded, broad-minded
85	illogical, irrational	rational, logical
86	foolish, having book knowledge	sensible, having common sense
87	prejudiced, subjective	objective, unprejudiced
88	practicing group or peer pressure	practicing independent thought
89	one-dimensional, pedantic	creative, inspired
90	opinionated, being a know-it-all	wise, discerning
91	practicing negative thinking	practicing positive thinking
92	cynical, pessimistic	optimistic, idealistic, being a visionary
93	anxious, distressed, worried	hopeful, assured, confident
94	unquiet, uneasy, impatient	patient, having sangfroid, having aplomb
95	intolerant, being a small person	tolerant, being a big person
96	fixed, rigid	open to change
97	hostile, lustful, hateful	loving, warm, intimate, gregarious
98	dull, boring, common	vital, full of life
99	hating others as self	loving others as self
100	resentful, grudging	forgiving, merciful

Number	IMMATURE	MATURE
101	self-absorbed, self-pitying	concerned for others, caring
102	self-indulgent, selfish	charitable, practicing liberality
103	idle, slothful, lazy	industrious, being a hard worker
104	vacillating, hesitating, procrastinating	doing it now
105	mocking, complaining	doing, expressing willpower
106	scoffing, thinking it awful	being part of the solution
107	envious, practicing low-mindedness	generous, kind
108	thieving, covetous	stewarding, guarding
109	equivocating, prevaricating	openhearted, straightforward
110	envious, unfaithful, jealous	trusting, faithful, having conviction
111	mistrustful, confused, doubtful	faithful, expecting
112	self-critical, self-abusing	self-nurturing, self-supporting
113	self-humiliating	accepting of criticism
114	exasperated, angry, having animosity	stable, unruffled, having poise
115	suspicious, self-doubting	confident, sure, positive
116	talebearing, gossiping, being a newsmonger	discretion, prudence
117	denying, un-accepting	accepting, affirming, recognizing
118	following worldly extremes	following the middle road, balance, equality
119	incompatible, inconsistent	consistent, compatible
120	careless, reckless	watchful, having foresight, practicing judgment
121	disorganized, chaotic, negligent	prepared, planning, ordered
122	wasting self-potential	self-actualizing
123	seeking self	seeking God
124	serving self-concepts	serving heart
125	serving self or mammon	serving God
126	serving idols, images	serving Spirit
127	dependent	resourceful

Middle Way or Synthesis Scale for Maturity

This scale is based on three positions or triality. There are two opposite ends with a point in-between them that contains or merges both of the opposites. (For more on and an expansion of triality, read World Within: The Inner Life.)

IMMATURE	MATURE	IMMATURE
thesis	synthesis	antithesis
codependent	independent	un-dependent
social closeness	social significance	social distance
dependent	interdependent	independent
passive	assertive	aggressive
submissive	balanced	dominant
self-identity	vessel identity	group identity
individualistic mentality	same but different mentality	collective mentality
separateness	share	belongingness, fusion
detached	aware	engulfed
centripetal	centered	centrifugal
focused on selfhood	ego-free	focused on relatedness
self-goals	spiritual goals	group goals
loyal to self	loyal to ideals	loyal to group
disengaged	detached	enmeshed
rigid boundaries	permeable boundaries	diffuse boundaries
chaotic	balanced	rigid
hectic	calm	fixed
morphogenic	original	morphostatic
changing, in-process	free	stuck, stable
talkative	moderate	reticent
selfish	sharing	unselfish
sadism	moderation	masochism
self-abasement	humility	vanity, self-love
experience	understanding, comprehension	knowledge

5 Thinking Positions Scale for Maturity

> When you correct your mind, everything else falls into place.
>
> —Lao Tzu

The *5 Thinking Positions* is a principle that teaches there are always five ways to think about anything. The 5 Thinking Positions provides for a more realistic view of reality and human behavior. (For more on the important principle of the 5 Thinking Positions, read *Games Ego Plays*.)

The table below reads from left to right, starting with immaturity increasing to maturity. The left middle, center, and right middle columns should be read as modifying the left end or the absolute immature style as it approaches the right end or the absolute mature style.

Left End	Left Middle	Center	Right Middle	Right End
irresponsible	frequently	occasionally	infrequently	responsible
undependable	often	sometimes	seldom	dependable
nonassertive	usually	half the time	rarely	assertive
conditioned	normally	now-n-then	a little	free
dependent	moderately	mildly	minimally	independent
fake	routinely	off and on	hardly ever	authentic
incongruent	quite a bit	somewhat	a little	congruent
un-integrated	generally	at times	seldom	integrated
immature	normally	now-n-again	infrequently	mature
inconsistent	routinely	now-n-then	rarely ever	consistent
dishonest	predominantly	half the time	scarcely	honest
irrational	as a rule	somewhat	a little	rational
unaware	mostly	sometimes	hardly	aware
lazy	often	occasionally	infrequently	industrious
mean	generally	half the time	a little	kind
stingy	often	somewhat	seldom	generous
unforgiving	moderately	mildly	minimally	forgiving
doubtful	often	sometimes	rarely	hopeful

Extrovert versus Introvert

Things may happen around you, and things may happen to you, but the only things that matter are the things that happen in you.

—Eric Butterworth

The "inner" is used to represent thoughts, feelings, sensations, memories, and any experiences that you might have in your mind, soul, or heart. The "outer" is used to represent events and experiences that you might have in or of the world your body moves in.

Simply put, "inner" is used to represent life inside the body, and "outer" is used to represent life outside the body.

This section uses the popular definition of introversion versus extroversion instead of the Jungian definition of those terms.

The introvert realizes that his or her inner is not his or her outer. The introvert interprets his or her outer through his or her inner so that the events of the outer are all either causing his or her inner or are occurring in relation to his or her preexisting inner.

The extrovert realizes his or her outer is not his or her inner. The extrovert interprets his or her inner through his or her outer so that the events of the inner are all either causing his or her outer or are occurring in relation to his or her preexisting outer.

The introvert holds the external as responsible for his or her feelings and thoughts even though the introvert recognizes the outer as separate. However, the introvert does not hold the world responsible for his or her situation. The introvert believes that he or she can control the outer but not his or her inner. The introvert makes his or her choices regarding the outer as he or she perceives what the outer's control and effect on his or her inner will be.

The extrovert holds the internal as responsible for his or her feelings and thoughts. However, the extrovert holds the world responsible for his or her situation. The extrovert believes that he or she can control his or her inner but not his or her outer. The extrovert makes his or her choices regarding the inner as he or she perceives what the inner's control and effect on his or her outer will be.

The introvert holds the world as responsible for his or her feelings and thoughts, but not for his or her actions, which he or she thinks are part of the world. The extrovert holds the world responsible for his or her actions, but not his or her feelings or thoughts, which he or she thinks is part of the world. Both types confuse self and reality, but in different ways.

So even though both types have some sanity, that sanity is, in practice, given up for his or her unsanity. We should draw on a person's sanity and strengthen so that it is not corrupted by his or her unsanity anymore, and then attack his or her unsanity head-on.

Some problems are the result of our being overly introverted or overly extroverted, and the characteristic responses that these positions lead to are often misdiagnosed as behavioral problems, psychodynamic problems, structural or systemic problems, or early childhood issues. While all or any of the above might have had a part in our forming an unbalanced style as an introvert or an extrovert—the problem is in the unbalance and not in the past history or present of our relationships.

KISS: Keep It Simple, Silly. We may be born with a predilection for either introversion or extroversion, but we can be balanced with either as dominant, as long as we draw upon the strengths of both to eliminate the weaknesses of both.

Table: REBT's ABCs of Emotions

In fairness, it should be noted that Adlerian Psychology was perhaps the first psychology to propose the direct relationship between thoughts and emotions. (See the writings of Rudolf Dreikurs.) For a philosophical argument in favor of the cognitive psychotherapy view of emotions being caused by thinking, see Robert C. Solomon's *The Passions*.

REBT and Cognitive Therapy (CT) are the two major forms of cognitive psychotherapy. Cognitive Behavioral Therapy (CBT) is the general term for therapies that are both cognitive and behavioral in nature, which includes REBT,

CT, and several others including the popular Dialectical Behavior Therapy (DBT).

(For more information on REBT, CT, and CBT: https://kevinfitzmaurice.com/lists-and-links/cbt-ct-rebt-cognitive-psychotherapies/.

For more information on REBT: https://kevinfitzmaurice.com/lists-and-links/links-to-websites-organized-by-topic/links-to-recommended-websites/rebt-website-links/)

Compare REBT's ABCs to "Stage 2: Stimulus-Thinking-Response (S-T-R)" in *C7: STPHFR Paradigm of Feeling Causation*.

REBT's ABCs of Emotions: A + B = C	
A	Attention paid to an event or experience.
B	Beliefs, interpretations, thoughts about A.
C	Consequences of A + B = feelings about A.
D	Dispute & challenge thoughts (B) about A.
E	Effect of disputing is finding new B about A.
F	Functional new feelings & responses to A.

Table: REBT's 11 Irrational Beliefs

The following eleven irrational beliefs are challenged as being self-defeating and self-disturbing as a part of the cognitive psychotherapy of Rational Emotive Behavior Therapy (REBT). In general, one of the major goals of REBT is to help people to think and act in less demanding ways, because demandingness is seen as self-defeating and self-disturbing.

11 Irrational Beliefs Challenged by REBT	
1	I must be loved by everyone, else I'm not lovable.
2	I must do everything well, else I am incompetent.
3	I must damn others if they do not treat me well.
4	I must damn life if things do not go well.
5	I must control events and people, because they control how I feel.
6	I must worry about anything fearful or risky.
7	I must avoid responsibilities and problems in order to be comfortable or content.
8	I must depend upon others, else my life or self will fall apart.
9	I must be controlled by my past and disturbed by anything that once disturbed me.
10	I must damn other's problems and be disturbed by them.
11	I must damn life if I cannot find the perfect answers to human problems.
These 11 irrational beliefs were rewritten, modified, and condensed from *Reason and Emotion in Psychotherapy, Revised and Updated* by Albert Ellis, Birch Lane Press, 1994.	
	https://kevinfitzmaurice.com

10 Types of Emotions

The ten types of emotions listed below are identified as the fundamental human emotions in *Human Emotions* by Carroll E. Izard. The terms after each emotion describe various ways that the emotions can manifest or be labeled.

1. **ANGER:** affronted, aggressive, annoyed, chafed, disturbed, enraged, exasperated, fuming, furious, galled, hateful, incensed, infuriated, irate, ireful, irritated, livid, negative, nettled, out of [one's] mind, outraged, peeved, perturbed, piqued to the core, pissed off, put out, raving, riled, smoking, ticked off, vengeful, vexed, violent, wrathful, wroth.

2. **CONTEMPT:** antagonistic, arrogant, critical, discarding, disclaiming, discomfited, discomposed, disconfirming, disconnected, discordant, discountenant, discounting, discouraging, discourteous, discrediting, discriminate, disdainful, disregarding, disrespecting, hateful, hostile, indignant, judgmental, loathful, mean, scornful, spiteful.

3. **DISGUST:** abhorring, averse, detestful, nauseated, offended, queasy, repelled, repugned, repulsed, revulsed, sickened, turned off, turned stomach.

4. **DISTRESS:** anguished, anxious, baffled, bewildered, confused, despairing, desperate, disappointed, discontented,

discouraged, diseased, fatalistic, flustered, frustrated, inadequate, nervous, out of place, tense, trapped, uncomfortable, uneasy, uptight.

5. FEAR: afraid, anxious, cautious, desperate, diffident, fearful, frantic, frightened, horrified, jealous, nervous, panicked, panicky, petrified, scared, suspicious, terrified, timid, worried.

6. GUILT: agonized, apologetic, burdened, condemned, dejected, demoralized, despondent, devastated, disconsolate, discouraged, disgraced, disheartened, forlorn, grieving, grievous, insecure, mournful, pitiful, regretful, rueful, sad, sorrowful, terrible, unhappy, woeful, wrong.

7. INTEREST: absorbed, advertent, attentive, concerned, curious, engrossed, excited, inquisitive, mindful, neutral, noticing, observant, thoughtful, watchful.

8. JOY: blessed, blissful, cheerful, compassionate, delighted, ecstatic, elated, enjoying, exalted, excited, free, fun, glad, happy, loved, marvelous, playful, pleased, positive, quietude, rapturous, religious, serene, spiritual, thrilled, tickled, tranquil, uplifted, willing.

9. SHAME: abandoned, agonized, alienated, ashamed, awkward, bashful, bewildered, bored, broken, chagrined, crushed, cut off, damaged, defeated, degraded, dejected, depressed, deserted, despised, discarded, disconcerted, dishonored, disliked, distraught, distressed, embarrassed, empty, forlorn, forsaken, friendless, helpless, hopeless, humbled, humiliated, hurt, inadequate, incapable, indifferent, inept, inferior, injured, isolated, lonely, lost, miserable, mortified, needy, not part of, outcast, overlooked, pained, perplexed, pierced, put down, rejected, shamed, shamefaced, shy, stung, tormented, tortured, unappreciated, unloved, unwanted, wounded.

10. SURPRISE: amazed, amused, astonished, astounded, dazzled, disoriented, dumbfounded, floored, pensive, perplexed, shocked, speechless, startled, stunned.

The Do's & Don'ts of Acceptance

In 1984, I spontaneously wrote the following list on acceptance to reinforce my new insight into acceptance. It is divided into two opposite positions, with equal emphasis on each.

The list came after I finally surrendered to the inviolability of the truth of emotional responsibility and became willing to learn to live by it. Emotional responsibility is still my guide and was the one answer that I had been missing in all my various pursuits for truth and peace. This principle has had a greater effect on my life than any other from Western psychology. My pursuit of emotional responsibility occurred mainly through the medium of REBT.

Do Accept from Self

• Accept all of your own feelings without prejudice. Be yourself.

• Accept total responsibility for all of your own feelings. Stop blaming others and being a martyr.

• Accept total responsibility for changing your own feelings. Become mature.

• Accept that other people have identical feelings to your own whether good or bad. Give up ego.

• Accept that everyone has good feelings. Have faith in people.

• Accept that you can encourage and help good feelings grow in others, with identical feelings in yourself. Love people.

• Accept that feelings are not right or wrong, true or false, facts, or things to be traced to a source; but feelings are either pro-life forces or pro-death forces, for things or people. Use life for life.

• Accept that things are not responsible for your good or bad feelings. Be objective.

Don't Accept from Others

- Don't accept any of the feelings of others as your own. Don't be others.

- Don't accept any responsibility for the feelings of others. Refuse all guilt for others.

- Don't accept any responsibility for changing the feelings of others. Let others mature.

- Don't accept anything others say that means their feelings are unique. Refuse to protect ego.

- Don't accept others' ideas that they don't have good feelings. Help others have faith.

- Don't accept that others can't help your good feelings grow with their identical ones. Let people love you.

- Don't accept any anti-life feelings for people or things. Refuse to server destruction.

- Don't accept things, places, events, or any outside force as responsible for your feelings or moods. Refuse subjectivity.

> Be not deceived; God is not mocked: for whatsoever a man soweth, that shall he also reap.
>
> —Galatians 6:7

2 Poems about Maturity

Poems can be understood as eliciting experience, emotion, and cognition. Many poems elicit a combination of these three elements. The highest poems focus on experience and the lowest poems focus on cognition. Anything can be called a poem that is written in a poetic form or style. The following two poems are of the lowest kind as they both focus on cognition.

I wrote the following poem in 1986 to represent the opposite of what we need to do.

Blame Game

Blame your mind for thinking what
your heart chose for it to magnify.
Blame your soul for sensing what thinking
your heart chose for it to record thereby.

Blame your body for wanting to do the evil
your heart chose for it to engage in.
Blame your sex for driving you to do what
your heart chose for it to begin.

Blame your pleasure for impelling you to the evil

your heart chose for you to commit.
Blame the joy of your senses for urging the evil
your heart chose for them as requisite.

Blame significant others for the feelings
your heart chose for you to feel.
Blame things and events for the moods
your heart chose for your inner meal.

Blame God or outside forces for the life script
your heart chose for your consequence.
Blame anything and everything for what
your heart in darkness chose for your sustenance.

I wrote the following poem in 1987 to represent the truth of emotional responsibility. Poetic forms are useful to both structure and condense ideas. This poem is in the poetic form known as a Villanelle.

Nothing Makes Me Feel Anything

I choose to feel something.
Response ability is the responder's.
Nothing makes me feel anything.

People say things to me meaning
one thing, and I interpret another.
I choose to feel something.

Events happen that are befitting
or not, I construe the encounter.
Nothing makes me feel anything.

You make me feel everything.
I won't admit I'm the assayer.
I choose to feel something.

No person is in me but me; blaming
others for my beliefs is where I err.
Nothing makes me feel anything.

The response is mine. Admitting
others are not my controllers,
I choose to feel easy-going.
Nothing makes me feel anything.

Final Insights

> There is nothing either good or bad but thinking makes it so.
>
> —William Shakespeare

3 Movie Examples

1. Intention Example: If you intended to enjoy and laugh at *A Night at the Opera*, then you probably found the movie amusing and funny. However, you might become more demanding of comedy films over time, intending to only enjoy those comedies that meet the highest standards. Therefore, another viewing of *A Night at the Opera* might find you thinking the movie was neither amusing nor funny.

2. Expectation Example: If you went to see the movie *Titanic* with overblown expectations, then you might not have even liked the movie. However, you might have lowered your expectations over time and decided that *Titanic* was a good Hollywood movie even if it was not a great film.

3. Interpretation Example: If you saw *Persona* and interpreted the movie to have profound meaning about social masks and identity issues in general, then you probably found the movie stimulating and exciting. However, after studying film criticism, you might have lowered your interpretation of the depth and meaning of the movie and now think of *Persona* in less fond and admiring ways.

Cause of Emotions

> The mind is its own place, and in itself can make a heaven of hell or a hell of heaven.
>
> —John Milton

The cause of emotions is choosing to experience something with your heart. People generally refer to this action as "taking something to heart." No one but you decides what you will take to heart. However, there are many powerful forces that push and prod you to take things to heart.

Here is a list of some feeling motivators, in order of their likely forcefulness over your choosing to experience them with your heart:

- self-identities
- self-evaluations
- self-stories
- insults from people whom you think know you
- looping, obsessing, or persistent thoughts

- strong demands or urges to control
- strong expectations
- dramatic experiences
- strong intentions
- strong desires
- strong bodily sensations
- strong external sensations
- considering something dangerous
- considering something important
- meaningful interpretations of events
- firm judgments
- strong beliefs
- powerful memories
- frequent thoughts
- intense thoughts

The order of the list of items that are directly tied to the cause of emotions is only an estimate. Each individual will have their own order for the items on the list, within the set amount of permutations available. The order of forcefulness for the items on the list can be changed by having some of the items connected to or dependent upon each other. Additionally, social, environmental, and physical influences can strengthen any one of the items, making it more irresistible. (For more on the nature of emotions, read FitzMaurice's ebooks *Attitude Is All You Need, Second Edition* and *Garden*.)

In section "7 Reasons for Emotional Responsibility" in chapter *What Is Maturity?*, some causes of feelings were stated that are not technically causes. Some items on the list were defined as causes because the human tendency to take such items to heart is almost automatic and therefore is predictable. For example, the practice of identifying with something causing feelings is technically inaccurate, because you do not have to experience with your heart all of your identifications of self as something. You can think about being some trait without necessarily having any feelings about being that trait.

However, it also true if you fully identify with something or someone then that will cause you to have feelings. Most of the time, people do take to heart what they identify with. Furthermore, only people who are self-aware are capable of making the fine distinctions between what they are identified with or what they are only intellectually or partially identified with. Therefore, the list of seven reasons for emotional responsibility works well for most people. In fact, most people would do well to be self-aware enough to directly experience the connection between three causes—their intentions, expectations, and interpretations—and the resulting feelings that they then have. (For an easy and effective system to learn to cope, manage, and relieve with your feelings, read FitzMaurice's Garden.)

Table: 12 Reasons Emotionally Responsible

12 Reasons: Emotional Responsibility	
1	I decide what I identify as self.
2	I decide to use ego or self-esteem.
3	I decide to listen to self-story or self-talk.
4	I decide to add feelings to feelings.
5	I decide to add experiences to feelings.
6	I decide to loop, obsess, or ruminate.
7	I decide to try to change or control things.
8	I decide to have expectations.
9	I decide to have or to engage desires.
10	I decide to make things important.
11	I decide to have beliefs & interpretations.
12	I decide to make claims & to know things.
From: *Secret of Maturity, Fourth Edition*	
Copyright © 2017 by Kevin Everett FitzMaurice https://kevinfitzmaurice.com	

Complicated STPHFR

It is possible to further complicate STPHFR to make it more accurate and precise. But such complications will only make it less accessible and palatable for the general population who are most in need of it.

For example, STPHFR can be extended by adding two more S's at the beginning. SSSTPHFR would be Stimulus Sensing Sensations Thinking Playback Hearting Feeling Response. Yes, there is first sensing of the stimulus, and that sensing must result in sensations else it is not sensing anything. Therefore SSSTPHFR is more accurate and precise than STPHFR.

Still, we need to clarify what is sensing and having the sensations. Hence, we would add Soul-Sensing and Soul-Sensations as the first option since heart sensing comes later in the model despite being a higher order of sensing than soul sensing. Next we would add Mind-Sensing and Mind-Sensations and then Body-Sensing and Body-Sensations because that is their order of relevance. This would still not be enough additions since sensing of various types occurs at other points along STPHFR as well. (For example, Mind-Sensing and Mind-Sensations occur at both T and P.) Furthermore, not every S elicits or is approached with every form of sensing but might be contacted by some and not others.

How about SSSSSTPHFR to represent the heart sensing the stimulus, the soul sensing the stimulus, the mind sensing the stimulus, and the body also sensing the stimulus before any thinking occurs? This is actually possible, and at younger ages it's more likely to occur. But we are again losing the usefulness of the simplicity of STPHFR though originally even plain STPHFR seems complex to most adults.

To be more accurate in the use of STPHFR, we should change hearting to mean sensing with the soul, not the heart. The heart senses energy, the soul senses sensations, and the mind senses forms (things, thoughts). And the STPHFR model is using the heart as if it was the soul and leaving out the function of the heart.

Indeed, there might come a time when humans have overcome emotional and intellectual immaturity to the point that a true accurate and scientific model of emotions and behavior can be used and studied. In the meantime, we had better oversimplify, use more acceptable terms, and use common understandings to reach the majority of people in the hopes of helping the human race to emotionally and intellectually evolve. The human race can currently claim technological advancement, but neither emotional nor intellectual advancement as a group. In fact, it is quite possible to argue that human emotional skills are devolving, not evolving. If you have any doubts about our devolving, follow politics or the news.

Share the Secret

> Things can never touch the soul, but stand inert outside it, so that disquiet can arise only from fancies within.
>
> —Marcus Aurelius Antoninus

Now you know the answer to the secret of maturity! Share what it means to be mature with everyone. Apply emotional maturity to your own life. Teach emotional responsibility to someone to learn it in a new and deeper way.

Remember, you can only be responsible for your own feelings, but you can also be responsible for the impact of what you do and say on the interpretations, vulnerabilities, and feelings of others. Congratulations on your choice to live a mature life.

Sometimes the person you know that most needs to grow up emotionally will only reject any advice or recommendations that you provide. Below is a strategy from the author's counseling practice that has had success in the past.

Mail a copy of the book you want your family member or friend to read to a friend who lives in different city, country, or state, then have your long-distance friend mail the book to your friend in need without any markings, letter, or a return address. Without knowing who sent the book or why, the book has more of a chance for being read by someone who resists advice or helpful suggestions.

Or, order it online and have it shipped directly to your friend in need. Be sure to use your friend's address as the return address, do not include a gift notice, and do not ask for a receipt. That way your friend should not be able to track the package.

The more a person needs help, the more likely that person will resist accepting or getting help. Why? Because such a person is invariably emotionally weak and vulnerable to such an extent that any confession of any fault will only lead to more ego pain and suffering. Avoiding and escaping ego pain is the life of the emotionally immature. Inflicting ego pain on others through criticism, gossip, sabotage, or sarcasm is the strategy of the emotionally immature who have discovered that such redirecting strategies are also effective strategies to avoid ego or emotional pain for themselves.

C9: Relevant Quotation Lists

More lists of quotations on topics such as acceptance, anger, anxiety, attitude, blaming, communication, coping, counseling, ego, failure, pride, semantics, school, self-esteem, thinking, work, and much more can be found on the author's website at:

https://kevinfitzmaurice.com/lists-and-links/quotations-topics/

The following lists of quotations are from the author's website and are current up to July 2017.

Quotations on Maturity

The quotations are organized alphabetically. Here is a link to the quotations on the author's website which might include new additions:

https://kevinfitzmaurice.com/lists-and-links/quotations-topics/quotations-maturity/

"A mature person is one who does not think only in absolutes, who is able to be objective even when deeply stirred emotionally, who has learned that there is both good and bad in all people and in all things, and who walks humbly and deals charitably with the circumstances of life, knowing that in this world no one is all knowing and therefore all of us need both love and charity." —Eleanor Roosevelt

"As you grow older, you stand for more and fall for less." —Anonymous"

"At twenty years of age, the will reigns; at thirty, the wit; and at forty, the judgment." —Benjamin Franklin

"By the time we hit fifty, we have learned our hardest lessons. We have found out that only a few things are really important. We have learned to take life seriously, but never ourselves." —Marie Dressler

"Conceit is a trait of an immoral person while modesty of a serious one." —Filo, fragment

"Education as growth or maturity should be an ever-present process." —Dewey

"Every calamity severs a string from the heart, until one scene of sorrow on the back of another matures us for eternity." —W. H. Brown

"From a timid shy girl I had become a woman of resolute character, who could no longer be frightened by the struggle with troubles." —Anna Dostoevsky

"Humility doesn't mean to think less of yourself, it means to think of yourself less." —Anonymous

"Humility is to make a right estimate of oneself." —Charles H. Spurgeon

"I believe that the sign of maturity is accepting deferred gratification." —Peggy Cahn

"I believe the first test of a truly great man is humility." —John Ruskin

"If people can't control their own emotions, then they have to start trying to control other people's behavior." Robin Skynner, noted psychiatrist

"It takes years and maturity to make the discovery that the power of faith is nobler than the power of doubt; and that there is a celestial wisdom in the ingenuous propensity to trust, which belongs to honest and noble creatures." —Harriet Beecher Stowe

"Man matures through work which inspires him to difficult good." —Pope John Paul II

"Mature means neither "too soon" nor "too late," but something between the two." —Publilius Nigidius

"Maturity arrives the day we don't need to be lied to about anything." —Frank Yerby

"Maturity begins to grow when you can sense your concern for others outweighing your concern for yourself." —John Maclaren

"Maturity comes when keeping a secret gives you more satisfaction than passing it along." —John M. Henry

"Maturity implies otherness . . . The art of living is the art of living with." —Julius Gordon

"Maturity is having the ability to escape categorization." —K. Rexroth

"Maturity is not being taken in by oneself." —K. von Schlaggenberg

"Maturity is not the absence of conflict, but knowing how to cope with it." —Anonymous

"Maturity is the ability to live in someone else's world." —Oren Arnold

"Maturity is the ability to postpone gratification." —Sigmund Freud

"Maturity is the capacity to endure uncertainty." —J. Finley

"Maturity is the high price of self-ownership." —Eli J. Schleifer

"Maturity is the slowness in which a man believes." —Baltasar Gracian

"Maturity is to face, and not evade, every fresh crisis that comes." —Fritz Kunkel

"Maturity is when we can treat ourselves in our own way rather than within the automatic ways of our parents in childhood." —Hugh Missildine

“Maturity is when you can sense your concern for others outweighing your concern for yourself.” —Anonymous

“Maturity is when you start to check on your illusions.” —Eugene E. Brussell

“People look with sympathetic eyes only at the blossom and the fruit, and disregard the long period of transition during which the one is ripening into the other.” —B. Auerbach

“Perfection is always found in maturity, whether it be in the animal or in the intellectual world. Reflection is the mother of wisdom, and wisdom the parent of success.” —James Fenimore Cooper

“Sound within silence, struggle within serenity, war within peace–these are the confusions that dissolve as the mind matures.” —Guggenheimer

“Taste is the mark of an educated man, imagination the sign of a productive man, and emotional balance the token of a mature man.” —Philip N. Youtz

"The cause of all sins in every case lies in the person's excessive love of self." —Plato, *Laws*

"The greatest treasure you can leave your children is a sense of modesty and the advice to follow virtuous persons." —Theognis

"The immature mind hops from one thing to another; the mature mind seeks to follow through." —Harry A. Overstreet

"The last part of a wise man's life is taken up in curing the follies, prejudices, and false opinions he had contracted in the former." —Jonathan Swift

"The mark of a mature man is the ability to give love and receive it joyously and without guilt." —Leo Baeck

"The process of maturing is an art to be learned, an effort to be sustained. By the age of fifty you have made yourself what you are, and if it is good, it is better than your youth." —Marya Mannis

"The turning point in the process of growing up is when you discover the core of strength within you that survives all hurt." —Max Lerner

"The willingness to forgive is a sign of spiritual and emotional maturity. It is one of the greater virtues which we should all aspire to develop." —Gordon B. Hinckley

"These possessions of a simpleton being the three I choose and cherish: to care, to be fair, to be humble." —Lao Tzu

"We allowed you a charade of trivial freedoms in order to avoid making those impositions on you that are in the end both the training ground and proving ground for true independence. We pronounced you strong when you were still weak in order to avoid taking part in the long, slow, slogging effort that is the only route to genuine maturity of mind and feeling. Thus, it was no small anomaly of your growing up that while you were the most indulged generation, you were also in many ways the most abandoned to your own meager devices by those into whose safe-keeping you had been given." —Midge Decter

"We have not passed that subtle line between childhood and adulthood until we move from the passive voice to the active voice–that is, until we have stopped saying 'It got lost,' and say, 'I lost it.'" —Sydney J. Harris

"What the old chew, the young spit out." —Yiddish proverb

"When I was a child, I spake as a child, I understood as a child, I thought as a child: but when I became a man, I put away childish things." —I Corinthians 13:11

"When Moses was grown up, he went unto his brethren, and looked on their burdens" [Exodus 2:11] How do we know that Moses was grown up? Because he went out unto his brethren, and was ready to bear the burdens and share the plight of his people. Maturity is sensitivity to human suffering." —Julius Gordon

"You grow up the day you have your first real laugh at yourself." —Ethel Barrymore

"Youth condemns; maturity condones." —Amy Lowell

Quotations on CBT, CT, & REBT

The quotations are organized alphabetically. Here is a link to the quotations on the author's website, which might include new additions:

https://kevinfitzmaurice.com/lists-and-links/quotations-topics/quotations-cbt/

For a complete system of Cognitive Behavioral Therapy (CBT), written for the average reader, discover *Garden*. To improve the efficiency and effectiveness of REBT theory and practice, discover *Not*.

• CBT = Cognitive Behavior Therapy. CT = Cognitive Therapy. REBT = Rational Emotive Behavior Therapy.

• CBT is the generalized form that contains portions of REBT, CT, and related practices.

• CT began with Aaron T. Beck and continues with its ongoing advocates and contributors.

• REBT began with Albert Ellis and continues with its ongoing advocates and contributors.

"A man is happy so long as he chooses to be happy and nothing can stop him." —Alexander Solzhenitsyn (1918–2008), Soviet writer and dissident

"A mature person is one who does not think only in absolutes, who is able to be objective even when deeply stirred emotionally, who has learned that there is both good and bad in all people and in all things." —Eleanor Roosevelt

"Although I am distinctly fallible and easily disturbable. I also have the ability to think, feel, and act differently and thus reduce my disturbance." —Albert Ellis

"A successful person is one who can lay a firm foundation with the bricks that others throw at him or her." —David Brinkley

"All human knowledge takes the form of interpretation." —Walter Benjamin

"All things are subject to interpretation whichever interpretation prevails at a given time is a function of power and not truth." —Friedrich Wilhelm Nietzsche

"Always remember this Anna, there are no walls, no bolts, no locks that anyone can put on your mind." —Otto Frank

"And above all, that the wrong-doer has done thee no harm, for he has not made thy ruling faculty worse than it was before." —Marcus Aurelius

"Buddhists were actually the first cognitive-behavioral therapists." —Jack Kornfield, *The Wise Heart: A Guide to the Universal Teachings of Buddhist Psychology*

"But do not of your own accord make your troubles heavier to bear and burden yourself with complaining." —Seneca

"But if anything in thy own disposition gives thee pain, who hinders thee from correcting thy opinion?" —Marcus Aurelius

“But I, unless I think that what has happened is an evil am not injured. And it is in power not to think so.” —Marcus Aurelius

“Change your thoughts and you change your world.” —Norman Vincent Peale

“Character is destiny.” —Heraclitus

“Consider how much more pain is brought on us by the anger and vexation caused by such acts than by the acts themselves, at which we are angry and vexed.” —Marcus Aurelius

“Constant attention by a good nurse may be just as important as a major operation by a surgeon.” —Dag Hammarskjold

“Despite everything, no one can dictate who you are to other people.” —Prince

"Don't ask why the patient is the way he is, ask for what he would change." —Milton Erickson

"Don't regard what anyone says of you, for this, after all, is no concern of yours." —Epictetus, *Enchiridion*

"Each morning when I open my eyes I say to myself: 'I, not events, have the power to make me happy or unhappy today. I can choose which it shall be. Yesterday is dead, tomorrow hasn't arrived yet. I have just one day, today, and I'm going to be happy in it.'" —Groucho Marx [Julius Henry], United States comedian

"Each of us does, in effect, strike a series of 'deals,' or compromises, between the wants and longings of the inner self, and an outer environment that offers certain possibilities and sets certain limitations." —Maggie Scarf

"Ellis' most recent writings propose that all emotional disturbance shares a single root: demandingness." —Walen, DiGiuseppe and Dryden, *A Practitioner's Guide to Rational Emotive Therapy, 2nd Edition,* p. 129

"Every man without passions has within him no principle of action, nor motive to act." —Claude Helvetius

"Everybody has their reasons." —Pierre-Auguste Renoir

"Everyone in a complex system has a slightly different interpretation. The more interpretations we gather, the easier it becomes to gain a sense of the whole." —Margaret J. Wheatley

"Everything can be taken from a man but one thing: the last of the human freedoms–to choose one's attitude in any given set of circumstances." —Victor E. Frankl (1905–1997), Austrian psychiatrist, *Man's Search for Meaning*

"Everything we hear is an opinion, not a fact. Everything we see is a perspective, not the truth." —Marcus Aurelius Antoninus, *Meditations*

"For who is he that shall hinder thee from being good and simple?" —Marcus Aurelius

"Give people the right to be wrong. They will exercise this right whether you give it to them or not." —Windy Dryden

"God grant me the serenity to accept the things I cannot change, courage to change the things I can, and the wisdom to know the difference. Living one day at a time; accepting hardships as the pathway to peace; taking as He did, this world as it is, not as I would have it. Trusting that He will make all things right IF I surrender to His will; that I may be reasonably happy in this life and supremely happy with Him, forever in the next." —Karl Paul Reinhold Niebuhr (1892–1971)

"Happiness depends on ourselves." —Aristotle

"Happiness does not depend on outward things, but on the way we see them." —Leo Tolstoy (1828–1910), Russian writer and philosopher

"Happiness is an inside job." —William Arthur Ward

“Happiness is a state of mind. It’s just according to the way you look at things.” —Walt Disney

“Happiness is an attitude. We either make ourselves miserable, or happy and strong. The amount of work is the same.” —Francesca Reigle

“Happiness is that state of consciousness which proceeds from the achievement of one’s values.” —Ayn Rand

“Happiness is when what you think, what you say, and what you do are in harmony.” —Mahatma Gandhi

“Happy is the man who early learns the wide chasm that lies between his wishes and his powers.” —Johann Wolfgang van Goethe

“He who has a ‘why’ to live for can bear with almost any ‘how’.” —Friedrich Wilhelm Nietzsche

"He who neglects what is done for what ought to be done, sooner effects his ruin than his preservation." —Machiavelli

"His own character is the arbiter of every one's fortune." — Publius Syrus (42 B.C.)

"I am not a product of my circumstance, I am a product of my decisions." —Steven Covey

"Identity is invariably false to facts." —Alfred Korzybski

"If my body is enslaved, still my mind is free." —Sophocles

"If you are distressed by anything external, the pain is not due to the thing itself but to your own estimate of it: and this you have the power to revoke at any moment." —Marcus Aurelius Antoninus (121–180), Roman philosopher and emperor

“If you change the way you look at things, the things you look at change.” —Wayne Dyer

“If you don’t like something, change it. If you can’t change it, change the way you think about it.” —Mary Engelbreit

“If you really want to be happy, nobody can stop you!” —Sister Mary Tricky

“If thou art pained by any external thing, it is not this thing that disturbs thee, but thy own judgment about it.” —Marcus Aurelius

“In order to be effective you need not only virtue but also mental strength.” —Aristotle, *Politics*

“It is much harder to live a life of freedom and self-rule than to be ruled by others.” —Mordechai Kaplan

“It is not men’s acts which disturb us, for those acts have their foundation in men’s ruling principles, but is our own opinions which disturb us.” —Marcus Aurelius

“It’s not what you look at that matters, it’s what you see.” — Henry David Thoreau

“Keep your thoughts positive because your thoughts become your words. Keep your words positive because your words become your behaviors. Keep your behaviors positive because your behaviors become your habits. Keep your habits positive because your habits become your values. Keep your values positive because your values become your destiny.” —Mohandas K. Gandhi

“Let us not burden our remembrances with a heaviness that is gone.” —William Shakespeare

“Life is 10% what happens to you and 90% how you handle what happens to you.” —Anonymous

"Life is never made unbearable by circumstances, but only by lack of meaning and purpose." —Viktor Frankl

"Life is what we make it, always has been, always will be." —Grandma Moses

"Make the best use of what is in your power, and take the rest as it happens." —Epictetus

"Man can alter his life by altering his thinking." —William James

"Man is not the creature of circumstances, circumstances are the creatures of men. We are free agents, and man is more powerful than matter." —Benjamin Disraeli

"Man is the artificer of his own happiness." —Henry David Thoreau

"Many persons have a wrong idea of what constitutes true happiness. It is not attained through self-gratification but through fidelity to a worthy purpose." —Helen Keller

"Men are disturbed not by things, but by the principles and notions which they form concerning things." —Epictetus

"Men are disturbed not by things, but by the view which they take of them." —Epictetus, Greek Stoic philosopher

"Most folks are as happy as they make up their minds to be." —Abraham Lincoln (1809–1865), American president

"Most people believe they see the world as it is. However, we really see the world as we are." —Anonymous

"Most powerful is he who has himself in his own power." —Seneca

"My one fear is that I will not be worthy of my sufferings." —Fyodor Mikhailovich Dostoyevsky (1821–1881), Russian writer

"Necessity is not an established fact, but an interpretation." —Friedrich Wilhelm Nietzsche (Compare to REBT on Shoulds)

"Needing leads to bleeding–to almost all inevitable suffering." —Albert Ellis, *Buddhism and Rational Emotive Behavior Therapy*

"Negative thinking is the highest form of intelligence." —Jiddu Krishnamurti (1895–1986), Indian philosopher, *Commentaries on Living, Second Series*, p. 71

"No one can make you feel inferior without your consent." —Eleanor Roosevelt

"Nobody can hurt me without my permission." —Mohandas K. Gandhi

“Nothing has meaning except for the meaning you give it.” —T. Harv Eker

“One who is too insistent on his own views, finds few to agree with him.” —Lao Tzu

“One who takes a calm and rational approach toward life.” —American Heritage dictionary definition of philosopher

“One will rarely err if extreme actions be ascribed to vanity, ordinary actions to habit, and mean actions to fear.” —Friedrich Wilhelm Nietzsche (1844–1900), German philosopher

“Our emotions are the result of our beliefs.” —Lie Yukou

“Our life is what our thoughts make it.” —Marcus Aurelius Antoninus, *Meditations, Book IV*

"Peace is the result of retraining your mind to process life as it is, rather than as you think it should be." —Wayne Dyer

"People don't just get upset. They contribute to their upsetness." —Albert Ellis

"Practice is everything." —Periander, *Lives of Eminent Philosophers* by Diogenes Laërtius

"Practice then from the start to say to every harsh impression, 'You are an impression, and not at all the thing you appear to be.' Then examine it and test it by these rules you have, and firstly, and chiefly, by this: whether the impression has to do with the things that are up to us, or those that are not; and if it has to do with the things that are not up to us, be ready to reply, 'It is nothing to me.'" —Epictetus

"Put from you the belief that 'I have been wronged', and with it will go the feeling. Reject your sense of injury, and the injury itself disappears." —Marcus Aurelius Antoninus, *Meditations, Book IV*

“Rejection is unpleasant, but not deadly.” —Albert Ellis

“Resolve to dismiss thy judgment about an act as if it were something grievous and thy anger is gone.” —Marcus Aurelius

“Rule your mind or it will rule you.” —Horace, Roman poet

“Speak and act from unwise thoughts, and sorrow will follow you as surely as the wheel follows the ox who draws the cart. Speak and act from wise thoughts and happiness will follow you as closely as your shadow, unshakeable.” —*Dhammapada*

“Sticks and stones will break my bones but words will never hurt me.” —Nursery rhyme

“Such as are they habitual thoughts, such also will be the character of thy mind; for the soul is dyed by the thoughts.” —Marcus Aurelius

"Take away thy opinion, and then there is taken away the complaint." —Marcus Aurelius

"That which does not kill me, makes me stronger." —Friedrich Wilhelm Nietzsche

"That which is evil to thee and harmful has its foundation only in the mind." —Marcus Aurelius

"The best way to define a man's character would be to seek out the particular mental or moral attitude in which, when it came upon him, he felt most deeply and intensely active and alive." —William James (1842–1910), American psychologist and philosopher

"The condition and characteristic of a vulgar person is that he never expects either benefit or hurt from himself, but from externals. The condition and characteristic of a philosopher is that he expects all hurt and benefit from himself." —Lucretius

"The depressed man lives in a depressed world." —Ludwig Wittgenstein (1889–1951)

"The description is not the described." —J. Krishnamurti

"The fact is one thing and the idea about the fact is another." —J. Krishnamurti

"The fault, Dear Brutus, is not in our stars; but in ourselves, that we are underlings." —William Shakespeare, *Julius Caesar*

"The greater part of our happiness or misery depends on our dispositions and not on our circumstances." —Martha Washington

"The greatest weapon against stress is our ability to choose one thought over another." —William James

"The happiness of your life depends upon the quality of your thoughts, therefore guard accordingly; and take care that you entertain no notions unsuitable to virtue, and reasonable nature." —Marcus Aurelius Antoninus

"The individual is taught that there is nothing that he as a total person is to feel ashamed of or self-hating for." —Albert Ellis, *Reason and Emotion in Psychotherapy Revised*

"The interpretation of our reality through patterns not our own, serves only to make us ever more unknown, ever less free, ever more solitary." —Gabriel Garcia Marquez

"The map is not the territory." —Alfred Korzybski

"The mind is its own place, and in itself can make a heaven of hell or a hell of heaven." —John Milton (1608–1674), English poet

"The most important decision you make is to be in a good mood." — Voltaire

“The origin of sorrow is this: to wish for something that does not come to pass.” —Epictetus, *Discourses*

“The present non-aristotelian system is based on fundamental negative premises; namely, the complete denial of ‘identity’.” —Alfred Korzybski (1879–1950), Polish-born American philosopher, *Science and Sanity,* page 10

“The relish of good and evil depends in a great measure upon the opinion we have of them.” —Michel Eyquem de Montaigne (1533–1592), French essayist

“The thought is not the thing.” —Alfred Korzybski

“The thought is not the thing.” —J. Krishnamurti

“The trouble with most therapy is it helps you feel better. But you don’t get better. You have to back it up with action, action, action.” —Albert Ellis

"The uncontrolled mind is to us as an enemy on the battlefield." —Krishna, to the Archer Arjuna, from *The Bhagavad Gita*

"The unexamined life is not worth living." —Socrates

"The wise man thinks about his troubles only when there is some purpose in doing so; at other times he thinks about others things." —Bertrand Russell (1872– 1970), British author, mathematician, and philosopher

"The world is what we make of it. We create our sorrows. If this is the case, why make problems for ourselves." —Lie Yukon

"There is no misery unless there be something in the universe which he thinks miserable." —Seneca

"There is nothing either good or bad but thinking makes it so." —William Shakespeare, *Hamlet, Act II, Scene 2*

"There is only one way to happiness and that is to cease worrying about things which are beyond the power of our will." —Epictetus

"Things can never touch the soul, but stand inert outside it, so that disquiet can arise only from fancies within." —Marcus Aurelius Antoninus, *Meditations, Book IV*

"Things may happen around you, and things may happen to you, but the only things that matter are the things that happen in you." —Eric Butterworth, Unity minister

"Think you can, think you can't; either way, you'll be right." —Henry Ford

"Thou are injuring thyself, my child." —Marcus Aurelius

"Thoughts are mightier than strength of hand." —Sophocles, *Phaedra*

“Thus the negative perception is the triumph of consciousness.” —Alfred North Whitehead, 1861-1947: British mathematician and philosopher

“To be wronged is nothing unless you continue to remember it.” —Confucius

“To every thing there is a season, and a time to every purpose under the heaven.” —Ecclesiastes 3:1

“To rule yourself is the ultimate power.” —Seneca

“Today I have got out of all trouble, or rather I have cast out all trouble, for it was not outside, but within and in my opinions.” —Marcus Aurelius

“Tragedy is in the eye of the observer, and not in the heart of the sufferer.” —Ralph Waldo Emerson

"Turn your mind away from things which are not permanent." —*Majjhima Nikaya*

"Unless one dream one's finest dreams in solitude, unless one reach the point of being able to dispense with all human company, all distraction, all traffic with the world–even the companionship of great souls and first-rate minds–unless one be self-sufficient, finding the first and best entertainment within oneself, within the depth of one's own person, one ought to sweep one's claims to greatness into one's pocket there accumulated, one ought to steal away out of the sacred presence of a nature to which one does not belong." —Johann Wolfgang Goethe (1749–1832), German writer, poet, and scientist

"Very little is needed to make a happy life; it is all within yourself, in your way of thinking." —Marcus Aurelius

"Watch your thoughts, for they become words. Watch your words, for they become actions. Watch your actions, for they become habits. Watch your habits, for they become your character. And watch your character, for it becomes your destiny." —Saying developed over time

“We are more often frightened than hurt; and we suffer more from imagination than from reality.” —Seneca

“We can actually put the essence of neurosis in a single word: blaming–or damning.” —Albert Ellis and Robert A. Harper, *A Guide to Rational Living, Third Edition,* p. 127

“We either make ourselves miserable, or we make ourselves strong. The amount of work is the same.” —Carlos Castaneda

“We must take care of our minds because we cannot benefit from beauty when our brains are missing.” —Euripides, fragment

“We often add to our pain and suffering by being overly sensitive, over-reacting to minor things, and sometimes taking things too personally.” —Dalai Lama

“We shall not cease from exploration and the end of all our exploring will be to arrive where we started and know the place for the first time." —Thomas Stearns Eliot (1888-1965), American-born British writer

"We should pledge ourselves to the proposition that the irresponsible life is not worth living." —Thomas S. Szasz (1920–2012), Hungarian-born American psychiatrist

"What has always made a hell on earth is that man has tried to make it his heaven." —Friedrich Holderlin

"What you believe you experience." —J. Krishnamurti, *Commentaries on Living, Volume 1,* p. 88

"Whatever a person frequently thinks and reflects on, that will become the inclination of their mind." —Buddha

"Whatever you say something is–it is not." —Alfred Korzybski

“When confronted with a situation which we cannot change, we are then challenged to change ourselves.” —Viktor Frankl

“When I am disturbed, it is because I find some person, place, thing, or situation–some fact of my life–unacceptable to me, and I can find no serenity until I accept that person, place, thing, or situation as being exactly the way it is supposed to be at this moment.” —*Alcoholics Anonymous, Third Edition* (the Big Book), p. 449

“When you correct your mind, everything else falls into place.” —Lao Tzu

“Whilst part of what we perceive comes through our senses from the objects around us, another part (and it may be the larger part) always comes out of our own head.” —William James

“With out thoughts we make the world.” —Gautama Buddha

“Words are the physicians of a mind diseased.” —Aeschylus, *Prometheus Bound*

“You can only be a ‘victim’ of yourself. It’s all how you discipline your mind.” —Epictetus

“You can’t step into the same river twice.” —Heraclitus

“You mainly feel the way you think.” —Albert Ellis, voted the second most influential psychologist of all time by the American Psychological Association (APA)

“You never truly need what you want. That is the main and thoroughgoing key to serenity.” —Albert Ellis, *Buddhism and Rational Emotive Behavior Therapy*

“Your worst enemy cannot harm you as much as your own unguarded thoughts.” —Buddha

Quotations on Responsibility

The quotations are organized alphabetically. Here is a link to the quotations on the author's website which might include new additions:

https://kevinfitzmaurice.com/lists-and-links/quotations-topics/quotations-responsibility/

"A baby expects to be soothed, but a mature adult soothes themselves." —Kevin Everett FitzMaurice

"A man is always responsible, whether his act is intentional or inadvertent, whether he is awake or asleep." —*Bava Qamma* 2:6

"A man of ability and the desire to accomplish something can do anything." —Donald Kircher

"A man's as miserable as he thinks he is." —Marcus Seneca

"A wise man will make more opportunities than he finds." —Francis Bacon

"Accuse not Nature, she hath done her part; Do thou but thine." —John Milton, *Paradise Lost*

"Adults are expert at self-disturbance and inept at self-soothing." —Kevin Everett FitzMaurice

"Always remember this Anna, there are no walls, no bolts, no locks that anyone can put on your mind." —Otto Frank

"An excuse is a lie guarded." —Jonathan Swift

"Are you part of the problem or part of the solution?" — Anonymous

"Be your own light. Be your own refuge. Confide in nothing outside of yourself. Hold fast to truth that it may be your guide. Hold fast to truth that it may be your protector." —*Mahaparinibbana Sutta*

"But let every man prove his own work, and then shall he have rejoicing in himself alone, and not in another." —Galatians 6:4

"Discipline is just choosing between what you want now and what you want most." —Anonymous

"Don't feel entitled to anything you don't sweat and struggle for." —Marian Wright Edelman (1939–)

"Don't go around saying the world owes you a living. The world owes you nothing. It was here first." —Mark Twain (1835–1910)

"Don't go around saying the world owes you a living. The world owes you nothing. It was here first." —Mark Twain

“Each man the architect of his own fate.” —Sallust

“Either do not attempt at all, or go through with it.” —Ovid

“For who is he that shall hinder thee from being good and simple?” —Marcus Aurelius

“Great works are performed not by strength, but by perseverance.” —Samuel Johnson

“He who conquers himself is mighty.” —Buddhist saying

“How does a person who cannot tame his desires differ from the most ignorant beast?” —Xenophon, *Memorabilia*

“I am happy and content because I think I am.” —Alain-Rene Lesage

“I am the master of my fate: I am the captain of my soul.” —W. E. Henley, *Invictus*

“I have always regarded myself as the pillar of my life.” —Meryl Streep

“I realized that they had already taken everything from me except my mind and my heart. Those they could not take without my permission. I decided not to give them away. And neither should you.” —Nelson Mandela

“If pleasure first, then pain second.” —Kevin Everett FitzMaurice

“If we have not peace within ourselves, it is in vain to seek it from outward sources.” —Francois de La Rochefoucauld

“If you would have a faithful servant, and one that you like, serve yourself.” —Benjamin Franklin

“In the councils of government, we must guard against the acquisition of unwarranted influence, whether sought or unsought, by the military-industrial complex. The potential for the disastrous rise of misplaced power exists and will persist." —Dwight D. Eisenhower, 1961, US President

"It is better to conquer yourself than to conquer a thousand others. Victory over others is a hollow gain, while victory over oneself is something not even the gods can take reverse." —*Dhammapada: The Thousands,* verses 103–105

"It is much harder to live a life of freedom and self-rule than to be ruled by others." —Mordechai Kaplan

"It is not easy to find happiness in ourselves, and it is not possible to find it elsewhere." —Agnes Repplier

"It is not in the stars to hold our destiny but in ourselves." —William Shakespeare

"It is not men's acts which disturb us, for those acts have their foundation in men's ruling principles, but is our own opinions which disturb us." —Marcus Aurelius

"It is only you who can master your self. But once this is done, it is a rare blessing." —*Dhammapada: Self,* verse 160

"It is the part of an uneducated person to blame others where he himself fares ill; to blame himself is the part of one whose education has begun; to blame neither another nor his own self is the part of one whose education is already complete." —Epictetus, *Enchiridion*

"Knowing yourself is the beginning of all wisdom." —Aristotle

"Life always gets harder towards the summit–the cold increases, responsibility increases." —Friedrich Wilhelm Nietzsche (1844–1900)

"Luck is where preparation meets opportunity." —Anonymous

"Man is condemned to be free; because once thrown into the world, he is responsible for everything he does." —Jean-Paul Sartre (1905–1980)

“Man must cease attributing his problems to his environment, and learn again to exercise his will–his personal responsibility in the realm of faith and morals.” — Albert Schweitzer

“Most folks are as happy as they make up their minds to be.” —Abraham Lincoln

“My philosophy is that not only are you responsible for your life, but doing the best at this moment puts you in the best place for the next moment.” —Oprah Winfrey

“No man will succeed unless he is ready to face and overcome difficulties and prepared to assume responsibilities.” —William Boetcker

“No one has ever gotten to anyone.” —Kevin Everett FitzMaurice

“No one is free, who is not master of himself.” —Pythagoras

“Nobody can bring you peace but yourself.” —Ralph Waldo Emerson

“Not flattered by praise, not hurt by blame.” —Buddhist saying

“Not in the shouts and plaudits of the throng, but in ourselves, are triumph and defeat.” —Henry Wadsworth Longfellow

“Nothing can bring you peace but yourself.” —Ralph Waldo Emerson (1803–1882)

“Nothing is at last sacred but the integrity of your own mind.” —Ralph Waldo Emerson (1803–1882)

“Nothing stops the man who desires to achieve. Every obstacle is simply a course to develop his achievement muscle. It’s a strengthening of his powers of accomplishment.” —Eric Butterworth

"Obstacles don't have to stop you. If you run into a wall, don't turn around and give up. Figure out how to climb it, go through it, or work around it." —Michael Jordan

"One of the strongest characteristics of genius is the power of lighting its own fire." —John Foster

"Pain is inevitable. Suffering is optional." —Anonymous

"Self command is the greatest command of all." —Seneca

"Self-control is the chief element in self-respect and self-respect is the chief element in courage." —Thucydides, *The History of the Peloponnesean War*

"Self-sufficiency is both a good and an absolute good." —Aristotle, *Politics*

"Sickness is a hindrance to the body, but not to your ability to choose, unless that is your choice. Lameness is a hindrance to the leg, but not to your ability to choose. Say this to yourself with regard to everything that happens, then you will see such obstacles as hindrances to something else, but not to yourself." —Epictetus, *Enchiridion*

"Some people create their own storms, then get upset when it rains." —Unknown

"Some pursue happiness, others create it." —Anonymous

"Take care of your body as if you were going to live forever; and take care of your soul as if you were going to die tomorrow." —Saint Augustine

"Teaching the principle of emotional responsibility can be one of the hardest tasks in REBT as clients may have habitually blamed others for their problems and now the therapist is pointing to the true source of their emotional problems–themselves." —Michael Neenan and Windy Dryden, *Rational Emotive Behavior Therapy: Advances in Theory and Practice,* p. 43

"The ability to accept responsibility is the measure of the man." —Roy Smith

"The best project that you will ever work on is you." —Anonymous

"The cause of all sins in every case lies in the person's excessive love of self." —Plato, *Laws*

"The farther behind I leave the past, the closer I am to forging my own character." —Isabelle Eberhardt

"The fault, Dear Brutus, is not in our stars; but in ourselves, that we are underlings." —William Shakespeare, *Julius Caesar*

"The more you are willing to accept responsibility for your actions, the more credibility you will have." —Brian Koslow

"The only disability in life is a bad attitude." —Scott Hamilton

"The only way to deal with an unfree world is to become so absolutely free that your very existence is an act of rebellion." —Albert Camus

"The U. S. Constitution doesn't guarantee happiness, only the pursuit of it. You have to catch up with it yourself." —Benjamin Franklin

"The willingness to accept responsibility for one's own life is the source from which self-respect springs." —Joan Didion

"There is an expiry date on blaming your parents for steering you in the wrong direction; the moment you are old enough to take the wheel, responsibility lies with you." —J.K. Rowling

"There is no dependence that can be sure but a dependence upon one's self." —John Gay

"There is no man so low that the cure for his condition does not lie strictly within himself." —Thomas L. Masson

"There's a victory and defeat–the first and best of victories, the lowest and worst of defeats–which each man gains or sustains at the hands not of another, but of himself." —Plato, *Protagoras*

"They always say time changes things, but you actually have to change them yourself." —Andy Warhol

"Thou are injuring thyself, my child." —Marcus Aurelius

"Thou must blame nobody." —Marcus Aurelius

"To win over your bad self is the grandest and foremost of victories." —Plato

"We either make ourselves miserable, or we make ourselves strong. The amount of work is the same." —Carlos Castenada

"What poison is to food, self-pity is to life." —Oliver C. Wilson

"Whatever may be, I am still largely the creator and ruler of my emotional destiny." —Albert Ellis and Robert A. Harper, *A Guide to Rational Living, Third Edition*, p. 252

"While they were saying among themselves it cannot be done, it was done." —Helen Keller

"Who is a hero? He who conquers his will." —*Pirkei Avot* 4:1

"Who is strong? One who overpowers his inclinations." —Ben Zoma, *Ethics of the Fathers*, 4:1

“Who ranks as the highest? One who does not harm anything. One who never retaliates. One who is always at peace regardless of the other person’s disposition.” —*Dhammapada: The Highest,* verses 405–406

“Why is it that people are willing to take responsibility for their happiness or mild sadness but not their severe disturbance or great unhappiness?–why ego of course!” —Kevin Everett FitzMaurice

“You are only as good as your word.” —Cecily Morgan

“You cannot escape responsibility by avoiding it today.” —Abraham Lincoln

“You have to do the work, no one can do it for you.” —*Dhammapada: The Right Way,* verse 276

“Your life is a result of the choices you make. If you don’t like your life, it is time for you to start making better choices.” —Robert Mugabe

Quotations on Solitude

The quotations are organized alphabetically. Here is a link to the quotations on the author's website which might include new additions:
https://kevinfitzmaurice.com/lists-and-links/quotations-topics/quotations-solitude/

"A man has to live with himself, and he should see to it that he always has good company." —Charles Evans Hughes

"A man is born alone and dies alone; and he experiences the good and bad consequences of his karma alone; and he goes alone to hell or the Supreme abode." —Chanakya

"A man should keep for himself a little back shop, all his own, quite unadulterated, in which he establishes his true freedom and chief place of seclusion and solitude." —Montaigne (1533–1592)

"A solitude is the audience chamber of God." —Walter Savage Landor

"A wise man never enjoys himself so much, nor a fool so little, as when alone." —Josh Billings (1818–1885)

"All the unhappiness of men arises from one single fact, that they cannot stay quietly in their own chamber." —Blaise Pascal (1623–1662)

"Alone, even doing nothing, you do not waste your time. You do, almost always, in company. No encounter with yourself can be altogether sterile: Something necessarily emerges, even if only the hope of some day meeting yourself again." —Emile M. Cioran

"And for this you must have quiet and solitude. But society does not allow you to have them. You must be with people, outwardly active at all costs. If you are alone you are considered antisocial or peculiar, or you are afraid of your own loneliness." —J. Krishnamurti, *The Collected Works of J. Krishnamurti, Volume III,* p. 216

"And Wisdom's self/ Oft seeks to sweet retired solitude/ Where with her best nurse Contemplation/ She plumes her feathers, and lets grow her wings." —John Milton (1608–1674)

“As for solitude, I cannot understand how certain people seek to lay claim to intellectual stature, nobility of soul and strength of character, yet have not the slightest feeling for seclusion; for solitude, I maintain, when joined with a quiet contemplation of nature, a serene and conscious faith in creation and the Creator, and a few vexations from outside is the only school for a mind of lofty endowment.” —Johann Wolfgang von Goethe (1749–1832)

“Be alone, that is the secret of invention; be alone, that is when ideas are born.” —Nikola Tesla

“Better be alone than in bad company.” —John Clark, 1596-1658

“By all means use sometimes to be alone [illegible] eorge Herbert

“Deep down, Erikson wants pr[illegible] respected and admired–and very deep dow[illegible] be left alone.” —Stanley Hoffmann

“Every man must do two things alone; he must do his own believing and his own dying.” —Martin Luther

“Flight of the alone to the Alone.” —Plotinus (205–270)

“For nowhere either with more quiet or more freedom from trouble does a man retire than into his own soul.” —Marcus Aurelius

“Friendship with oneself is all-important, because without it one cannot be friends with anyone else.” —Eleanor Roosevelt

“[illegible] you[illegible]ay from the crowd when you can. Keep yourself to [illegible]f only for a few hours daily.” —Arthur Brisbane

“Give up [illegible] solitude a[illegible] [illegible]ide and be in the light. Seek happiness in [illegible] material pleasures.” —*Dhammapada: The Wise P*[illegible] [illegible]7

“Give up the dark side and be in the light. Seek happiness in solitude and not in material pleasures.” —*Dhammapada: The Wise Person,* verse 87

“God created man and, finding him not sufficiently alone, gave him a companion to make him feel his solitude more keenly.” —Paul Valéry (1871–1945)

“Great decisions in the realm of thought and momentous discoveries and solutions of problems are only possible to an individual working in solitude.” —Sigmund Freud (1856–1939)

“He who delights in solitude is either a wild beast or a god.” —Friedrich Nietzsche (1813–1855)

“‘He who seeks may easily get lost himself. It is a crime to go apart and be alone.’–Thus speaks the herd.” —Friedrich Nietzsche (1813–1855)

“How sweet, how passing sweet, is solitude!” —Jean De La Bruyère (1645–1696)

"I find it wholesome to be alone the greater part of the time … I love to be alone. I never found the companion that was so companionable as solitude. We are for the most part more lonely when we go abroad among men than when stay in our chambers. A man thinking or working is always alone, let him be where he will." —Henry David Thoreau (1817–1862)

"I had three chairs in my house: one for solitude, two for friendship, three for society." —Henry David Thoreau (1817–1862)

"I have never found a companion that was so companionable as solitude. We are for the most part more lonely when we go abroad among men than when we stay in our chambers. A man thinking or working is always alone, let him be where he will." —Henry David Thoreau (1817–1862)

"I have to be alone very often. I'd be quite happy if I spent from Saturday night until Monday morning alone in my apartment. That's how I refuel." —Audrey Hepburn

“I hold this to be the highest task for a bond between two people: that each protects the solitude of the other.” —Rainer Maria Rilke (1875–1926)

“I live in that solitude which is painful in youth, but delicious in the years of maturity.” —Albert Einstein (1879–1955)

“I lived in solitude in the country and noticed how the monotony of a quiet life stimulates the creative mind.” —Albert Einstein (1879–1955)

“I love tranquil solitude.” —Percy Bysshe Shelly (1792–1822)

“I only go out to get me a fresh appetite for being alone.” —Lord Byron (1788–1824)

“I restore myself when I’m alone.” —Marilyn Monroe

“I think it’s very healthy to spend time alone. You need to know how to be alone and not defined by another person.” —Oscar Wilde

“I was never less alone than when by myself.” —Edward Gibbon (1737–1794)

“I went to the woods because I wished to live life deliberately, to confront only the essential facts of life, and see if I could not learn what it had to teach, and not, when I came to die, discover that I had not lived.” —Henry David Thoreau (1817–1862)

“If we are to survive, we must have ideas, vision, courage. There things are rarely produced by communities. Everything that matters in our intellectual and moral life begins with an individual confronting his own mind and conscience in a room by himself.” —Arthur M. Schlesinger, Jr. (1971–)

“If you are afraid of being lonely, don’t try to be right.” — Jules Renard

"If you are lonely when you're alone, you are in bad company." —Jean-Paul Sartre

"If you are not enough company, then no amount of people can ever be enough company–after all–they are just more you." —Kevin Everett FitzMaurice

"If you cannot find a good companion to walk with, walk alone, like an elephant roaming the jungle. It is better to be alone than to be with those who will hinder your progress." —*Dhammapada: The Elephant,* verses 329–330

"If you don't like being in your own company, what makes you think others will?" —Anonymous

"If you make friends with yourself you will never be alone." —Maxwell Maltz

"In solitude, be a multitude to thyself." —Tibullus (54?–18? B.C.)

"In the tumult of great events, solitude was what I hoped for. Now it is what I love. How is it possible to be contented with anything else when one has come face to face with history?" —Charles de Gaulle (1890–1970)

"It is easy in the world to live after the world's opinion; it is easy in solitude to live after our own; but the great man is he who in the midst of the crowd keeps with perfect sweetness the independence of solitude." —Ralph Waldo Emerson (1803–1882)

"It may be laid down as a position which seldom deceives, that when a man cannot bear his own company, there is something wrong." —Samuel Johnson (1790–1884)

"Language... has created the word 'loneliness' to express the pain of being alone. And it has created the word 'solitude' to express the glory of being alone." —Paul Tillich

"Look within. Within is the fountain of good, and it will ever bubble up, if thou will ever dig." —Marcus Aurelius

"Men fear silence as they fear solitude, because both give them a glimpse of the terror of life's nothingness." —André Maurois

"Nature has made us a present of a broad capacity for entertaining ourselves apart, and often calls us to do so, to teach us that we owe ourselves in part to society, but in the best part to ourselves." —Montaigne (1533–1592)

"Never less alone than when alone." —Samuel Rogers (1763–1855)

"No one can help us to achieve the intimate isolation by which we find our secret worlds, so mysterious, rich and full. If others intervene, it is destroyed. This degree of thought, which we attain by freeing ourselves from the external world, must be fed by the inner spirit, and our surroundings cannot influence us in any way other than to leave us in peace." —Maria Montessori (1870–1952)

"No one with a mind is ever bored or lonely." —Kevin Everett FitzMaurice

“Not in the shouts and plaudits of the throng, but in ourselves, are triumph and defeat.” —Henry Wadsworth Longfellow

“Now the New Year reviving old Desires / The thoughtful Soul to Solitude retires.” —Edward FitzGerald (1809–1883)

“Oh blessed a thousand times the peasant who is born, eats and dies without anybody bothering about his affairs.” —Giuseppe Verdi

“‘On the whole, the longing for solitude is a sign that there still is spirit in a person and is a measure of what spirit there is.” —Søren Kierkegaard (1844–1900)

“One man runs to his neighbor because he is looking for himself, and another because he wants to loose himself. Your bad love of yourselves makes solitude a prison for you.” —Friedrich Nietzsche (1844–1900)

“One of the greatest necessities in America is to discover creative solitude.” —Carl Sandburg (1878–1967), American writer

“Our language has wisely sensed the two sides of man’s being alone. It has created the word ‘loneliness’ to express the pain of being alone. And it has created the word ‘solitude’ to express the glory of being alone.” —Paul Tillich (1886–1965)

“People who take time to be alone usually have depth, originality, and quiet reserve.” —John Miller

“Religion … shall mean for us the feelings, acts, and experiences of individual men in their solitude.” —William James (1842–1910)

“She would not exchange her solitude for anything. Never again to be forced to move to the rhythms of others.” —Tillie Olsen (1913–2007)

"Sit alone. Sleep alone. Travel alone. Do your practice alone. Enjoy your seclusion without desire." —*Dhammapada: Other Things,* verse 305

"Solitude either develops the mental power, or renders men dull and vicious." —Victor Hugo

"Solitude gives birth to the original in us, to beauty unfamiliar and perilous–to poetry. But also, it gives birth to the opposite: to the perverse, the illicit, the absurd." —Tomas Mann

"Solitude is as needful to the imagination as society is wholesome for the character." —James Russell Lowell (1819–1891)

"Solitude is naught and society is naught. Alternate them and the good of each is seen." —Ralph Waldo Emerson (1803–1882)

"Solitude is the place of purification." —Martin Buber (1878–1965)

"Solitude lies at the lowest depth of the human condition. Man is the only being who feels himself to be alone and the only one who is searching for the Other." —Octavio Paz (1941–1998)

"Solitude sometimes is best society / And short retirement urges sweet return." —John Milton (1608–1674)

"Solitude vivifies; isolation kills." —Joseph Roux (1834–1886)

"Solitude, the safeguard of mediocrity, is to genius the stern friend." —Ralph Waldo Emerson (1803–1882)

"Something of the hermit's temper is an essential element in many forms of excellence, since it enables men to resist the lure of popularity, to pursue important work in spite of general indifference or hostility, and arrive at opinions which are opposed to prevalent errors." —Bertrand Russell (1872–1970)

"Talent develops in quiet places." —Johann Wolfgang von Goethe (1749–1832)

"That inward eye/ Which is the bliss of solitude." —William Wordsworth (1770–1850)

"The best thinking has been done in solitude. The worst has been done in turmoil." —Thomas Alva Edison

"The departure from the world is regarded not as a fault, but as the first step into that noble path at the remotest turn of which illumination is to be won." —Joseph Campbell (1904–1987)

"The individual has always had to struggle to keep from being overwhelmed by the tribe. If you try it, you will be lonely often, and sometimes frightened. But no price is too high to pay for the privilege of owning yourself." —Friedrich Nietzsche (1844–1900)

"The nurse of full-grown souls is solitude." —James Russell Lowell (1819–1891)

“The only real progress lies in learning to be wrong all alone.” —Albert Camus

“The physical union of the sexes … only intensifies man’s sense of solitude.” —Nicolas Berdyaev

“The right to be let alone is the most comprehensive of rights and the right most valued in civilized man.” —Justice Louis D. Brandeis

“The secret of solitude is that there is no solitude.” —Joseph Cook

“The young should early be trained to bear being left alone; for it is a source of happiness and peace of mind.” —Arthur Schopenhauer (1788–1860)

“There is no free society without silence, without the internal and external spaces of solitude in which the individual freedom can develop.” —Herbert Marcuse (1898–1979)

“There is not true intimacy between souls who do not know how to respect one another’s solitude.” —Thomas Merton (1915–1968)

“There is pleasure in the pathless woods/ There is rapture on the lonely shore/ There is society, where none intrudes, by the deep sea and music in its roar/ I love not man the less, but Nature more.” —Lord Byron

“They are never alone that are accompanied [by] noble thoughts.” —Sir Philip Sidney (1554–1584)

“This great misfortune—to be incapable of solitude.” —Jean De La Bruyère (1645–1696)

“Those who would not be alone are those who are not worthwhile company.” —Kevin Everett FitzMaurice

“‘Tis solitude should teach us how to die; It hath no flatterers; vanity can give, No hollow aid; alone–man with God must strive.” —Lord Byron (1788–1824)

“To be lonely when alone means that you need others to feel alive, real, worthwhile—you alone are not enough.” —Kevin Everett FitzMaurice

“To be single is neither a crime against nature nor the state.” —Kevin Everett FitzMaurice

“To fear to be alone is to fear the company of oneself.” —Kevin Everett FitzMaurice

“To go into society, a man needs to retire as much from his chamber as from society. I am not solitary while I read and write, though nobody is with me. But if a man would be alone, let him look at the stars.” —Ralph Waldo Emerson (1803–1882)

“We’re all of us sentenced to solitary confinement inside our own skins, for life!” —Tennessee Williams (1911–1983)

“What a commentary on our civilization, when being alone is considered suspect; when one has to apologize for it, make excuses, hide the fact that one practices it–like some secret vice!” —Ann Morrow Lindbergh (1907–2001)

“What do you think is better: to seek for a partner, or to seek for the Self?” —*Buddhacarita*

“What lies behind us and what lies before us are tiny matters compared to what lies within us.” —Ralph Waldo Emerson (1803–1882)

“Who knows the world lives alone.” —Ali (600?–661)

“Whosoever delighted in solitude is either a wild beast, or a god.” —Aristotle (384–322 B.C.)

“You alone are enough for you.” —Kevin Everett FitzMaurice

"You cannot be lonely if you like the person you're alone with." —Wayne Dyer

"Your solitude will be a support and a home for you, even in the midst of very unfamiliar circumstances, and from it you will find all your paths." —Rainer Maria Rilke

End

Please visit the author's website: www.kevinfitzmaurice.com. There you will find free information and methods for peaceful living on more than six hundred webpages. Additionally, you will find a link page directing you to many other useful websites such as websites offering free education and non-violent revolution.

About the Author

Be it as a person's counselor or as a founding member of facilities for the homeless, Kevin Everett FitzMaurice, M.S., NCC, CCMHC, LPC, seeks to make others' lives better by helping others improve how they function. As a volunteer, he supports community services to improve others' living conditions. As a counselor, he *counsels* in the traditional sense: advising, directing, and nudging—or pushing—others into facing and resolving their issues.

Mr. FitzMaurice has a variety of formal and advanced training in counseling, which includes Addictions Counseling, Family Therapy, advanced Rational Emotive Behavior Therapy (REBT), Transactional Analysis (TA), and over 1300 hours of diverse training for continuing education units (CEUs). To make the best use of that extensive training, he takes an integrative approach, grounding himself in Cognitive Behavioral Therapy (CBT) and using the other theories to build upon that one core theory, rather than focusing on multiple theories and mastering none of them.

After more than twenty years in counseling, Mr. FitzMaurice has worked in the substance abuse field, directed two community mental health programs, and spent many years counseling in private practice. In that time, he has refined many principles for and methods of counseling. He now puts those principles and methods into book form to share them with a wider audience, so more people can benefit than he can reach in person. Currently, he has more than twenty-five books written, most of which are available worldwide as e-books from Amazon, Barnes&Noble, Google, Kobo, and Apple.

The philosophical odyssey of Mr. FitzMaurice began in the late '60s. It has remained a mostly self-taught pursuit, with little formal training or education in philosophy. The odyssey started with Western philosophy and a study of pragmatism and atheism. For example, he read every work of Nietzsche that had been translated into English at that time. From there, he moved to the study of Zen, Buddhism, Hinduism, and a misguided experimentation with psychedelics to achieve states of superconsciousness. He continued into Eastern philosophy, pursuing Taoism and J. Krishnamurti. Next came a study of Christianity that consisted of seven readings of the Old Testament and nine readings of the New Testament from cover to cover. This was followed by a formal study of Western psychology. The ongoing influences for FitzMaurice's thinking continue to be Christianity, General Semantics, Cognitive Behavioral Therapy (CBT), and an Eastern combination of J. Krishnamurti, Taoism, and Zen.

Academic Credentials: Master of Science (M.S.) in guidance and counseling, with a specialization in agency counseling, from the University of Nebraska. Associate of applied science in human services - chemical dependency counseling (with honors), from Metropolitan Community College.

National Certifications: National Certified Counselor (NCC); Certified Clinical Mental Health Counselor (CCMHC); Family Certification in REBT; Primary Certification in REBT; and Advanced Certification in REBT.

State Licensure: Licensed Professional Counselor (LPC) in Oregon; previously Licensed Independent Mental Health Practitioner (LIMHP) in Nebraska; previously Licensed Mental Health Counselor (LMHC) in Iowa.

Community Service: One of the original founders of the Francis House, Siena House, and Stephen Center homeless facilities still in operation in Nebraska. Supporter of the following charities: OxFam America, Amnesty International USA, Habitat for Humanity, and Green Peace. Organizer of free yoga classes in his local community.

Books Recommended by Usage

1. Discover Emotional Responsibility

The first step on the path to sanity is emotional responsibility.

To begin your understanding of emotional responsibility, read *The Secret of Maturity, Third Edition*.

To advance your understanding of emotional responsibility, read *Garden*.

If you want to focus on your attitude and emotional responsibility, then read *Attitude Is All You Need! Second Edition*.

Garbage Rules is about emotional responsibility for those stuck in drama games as a lifestyle. If you or your family is stuck in a cycle of dealing with social services or the criminal system, then this is a must read book for you. This book is also appropriate for those in early recovery and 12-step groups.

If you want to advance your counseling skills regarding emotional responsibility, then read both *Garden* and *Not*.

2. Discover Ego Domination

The second step on the path to sanity is to recognize ego as the problem in all things.

To begin to understand how ego is your problem, read *Ego*. This book requires you to be aware of your self-talk (inner dialogue). To become more aware of your self-talk, first read *Garden*.

To support and reinforce the work you learn to practice in *Ego*, read both *What's Your Story?* and *Journal Journey from Ego*.

To gain more insight into the false beliefs and thinking errors of self-esteem and ego, read *Planet Earth: Insane Asylum for the Universe, Second Edition*.

To understand ego in social relationships, read *Games Ego Plays*.

To develop greater insight into ego and skills in spotting ego, read *Ego Playground*.

3. Discover Authentic Self

The third step is to strengthen your understanding of your original nature by reading *Self: Who Am I?*

4. Coping & Problem-Solving Skills

Coping and problem-solving skills are needed at every stage of the path to sanity. We are not born with these skills and few of us have been formally taught them. Therefore it is logical and practical to pursue a more complete understanding of them.

Stress for Success, Second Edition will help you to learn how to make stress work for you instead of against you.

Breathe will give you easy and simple exercises to instantly calm and center yourself in any situation.

Garden will teach you advanced coping skills that you can practice until they become habits.

Free Heart will teach you about your inner life and how to make it work and keep it working positively and productively.

Not addresses the underlying problem why coping and problem-solving fail.

5. Supporting Works for Steps

Other books support and reinforce the learnings about emotions, ego, and self in various ways.

We're All Insane! Second Edition will help you to understand and apply General Semantics principles to your practice of recognizing, removing, and replacing your ego.

Other titles are collections of ideas and sayings that help you to understand all of these principles from different perspectives and through different expressions. These include *Acid Test*, *Anything Goes*, *Something For Nothing* and books in the *3D: Daily Dose of Discernment* series.

6. Miscellaneous Works

Carl Rogers, Control Freak is for professional counselors interested in applying Carl Rogers's main technique.

How to Govern Anything is for those who want to discover and practice a saner system of governing any size organization or country.

Other Languages than English

Though inconvenient, it is possible to read FitzMaurice's books in languages other than English on your Kindle Paperwhite or Kindle (7th Generation). For more information, visit Kindle Paperwhite Support.

Recommended Books, Alphabetically by Author

The majority of the following books are recommended for the purposes of study and reference. Some books are listed only for reference purposes. The most profitable suggestions are Kierkegaard, Korzybski, Ellis, Krishnamurti, and Lao Tzu. Kierkegaard for true Christianity, which currently is the rarest thing on Planet Earth. Korzybski for detaching from your thoughts as reality or knowing. Ellis for basic and practical psychological strategies. Krishnamurti for understanding Eastern psychology and meditation. Lao Tzu for understanding the way of Spirit.

Alcoholics Anonymous World Services, Inc. *Alcoholics Anonymous: The Big Book, 3rd Edition*. Alcoholics Anonymous World Services, Inc., New York. 1939, 1955, 1976.

Barna, George. *The Second Coming of the Church*. Thomas Nelson, Nashville. 1998.

Beck, Aaron T., Rush, A. John, Shaw, Brian F., and Gary Emery. *Cognitive Therapy of Depression: A Treatment Manual*. Guilford Press, New York. 1979.

Benson, Herbert. *The Relaxation Response*. Avon Books, New York. 1975.

Berlinski, David. *The Devil's Delusion: Atheism and its Scientific Pretensions*. Basic Books, New York. 2009.

Berne, Eric. *Games People Play*. Ballantine Books, New York. 1964.

Borcherdt, Bill. *You Can Control Your Feelings! 24 Guides to Emotional Well-Being*. Professional Resource Exchange, Sarasota, FL. 1993.

Bynner, Witter. *The Way of Life According to Lao Tzu*. Putnam Publishing, New York. 1944.

Capra, Fritjof. *The Tao of Physics: Third Edition, Expanded*. Shambhala, Boston. 1991.

Csikszentmihalyi, Mihaly. *Living with Flow*. Nightingale Conant, Niles, IL. 1994.

Dryden, Windy. *Dealing With Anger Problems: Rational-Emotive Therapeutic Interventions*. Professional Resource Exchange, Sarasota, Florida. 1990.

Duncan, Ronald and Miranda Weston-Smith editors. *The Encyclopedia of Ignorance: Everything you ever wanted to know about the unknown*. Pergamon Press, Elmsford, NY. 1977.

Ellis, Albert. "RET Abolishes Most of the Human Ego." *Psychotherapy: Theory, Research and Practice*. 13:4, 343-348. 1976. Reprint available from the Albert Ellis

Institute, 45 East 64th Street, New York, NY. 10021-6593. (212) 535–0822.

Ellis, Albert. *Reason and Emotion in Psychotherapy, Revised and Updated*. Carol Publishing, New York. 1994.

Ellis, Albert. *How to Control Your Anxiety Before It Controls You*. Carol Publishing Group, Secaucus, NJ. 1998.

Ellis, Albert. *Feeling Better, Getting Better, Staying Better: Profound Self-Help for Your Emotions*. Impact Publishers, Atascadero, CA. 2001.

Ellis, Albert. *The Myth of Self-esteem: How Rational Emotive Behavior Therapy Can Change Your Life Forever.* Prometheus, Amherst, NY. 2005.

Ellis, Albert, and Windy Dryden. *The Practice of Rational-Emotive Therapy (RET)*. Springer, New York. 1987.

Ellis, Albert, and Robert A. Harper. *A Guide to Rational Living, Third Edition*. Wilshire Book Company, North Hollywood, CA. 1997.

Ellis, Albert, and Raymond C. Tafrate. *How to Control Your Anger Before It Controls You*. Kensington Publishing, New York. 1997.

FitzMaurice, Kevin Everett. *Self-Concept: The Enemy Within*. PalmTree Publishers, Omaha, NE. 1989.

FitzMaurice, Kevin Everett. *The Seventh Way: How to Live Beyond Self-Concepts*. PalmTree Publishers, Omaha, NE. 1990.

FitzMaurice, Kevin Everett. *Beyond Thought and Feeling: Meditation and the Structure of the Ego*. PalmTree Publishers, Omaha, NE. 1990.

FitzMaurice, Kevin Everett. *Planet Earth: Insane Asylum for the Universe—The First Report to the 2000 High Council*. PalmTree Publishers, Omaha, NE. 2000.

FitzMaurice, Kevin Everett. *Breathe*. FitzMaurice Publishers, Omaha, NE. 2010. Available for computers, smartphones, tablets, and e-readers from Amazon, Barnes & Noble, Google, Kobo, and Apple.

FitzMaurice, Kevin Everett. *Garden*. FitzMaurice Publishers, Omaha, NE. 2010. Available for computers, smartphones, tablets, and e-readers from Amazon, Barnes & Noble, Google, Kobo, and Apple.

FitzMaurice, Kevin Everett. *Not*. FitzMaurice Publishers, Omaha, NE. 2011. Available for computers, smartphones, tablets, and e-readers from Amazon, Barnes & Noble, Google, Kobo, and Apple.

FitzMaurice, Kevin Everett. *Ego*. FitzMaurice Publishers, Omaha, NE. 2011. Available for computers, smartphones, tablets, and e-readers from Amazon, Barnes & Noble, Google, Kobo, and Apple.

FitzMaurice, Kevin Everett. *Something For Nothing*. FitzMaurice Publishers, Omaha, NE. 2011. Available for computers, smartphones, tablets, and e-readers from Amazon, Barnes & Noble, Google, Kobo, and Apple.

FitzMaurice, Kevin Everett. *Anything Goes*. FitzMaurice Publishers, Omaha, NE. 2011. Available for computers, smartphones, tablets, and e-readers from Amazon, Barnes & Noble, Google, Kobo, and Apple.

FitzMaurice, Kevin Everett. *Acid Test*. FitzMaurice Publishers, Omaha, NE. 2011. Available for computers, smartphones, tablets, and e-readers from Amazon, Barnes & Noble, Google, Kobo, and Apple.

FitzMaurice, Kevin Everett. *Attitude Is All You Need! Second Edition*. FitzMaurice Publishers, Omaha, NE. 1997, 2011. Available for computers, smartphones, tablets, and e-readers from Amazon, Barnes & Noble, Google, Kobo, and Apple.

FitzMaurice, Kevin Everett. *3D: Daily Does of Discernment: 2005*. FitzMaurice Publishers, Omaha, NE. 2011. Available for computers, smartphones, tablets, and e-readers from Amazon, Barnes & Noble, Google, Kobo, and Apple.

FitzMaurice, Kevin Everett. *3D: Daily Does of Discernment: 2003-4*. FitzMaurice Publishers, Omaha, NE. 2012. Available for computers, smartphones, tablets, and e-readers from Amazon, Barnes & Noble, Google, Kobo, and Apple.

FitzMaurice, Kevin Everett. *Carl Rogers, Control Freak*. FitzMaurice Publishers, Omaha, NE. 2012. Available for computers, smartphones, tablets, and e-readers from Amazon, Barnes & Noble, Google, Kobo, and Apple.

FitzMaurice, Kevin Everett. *We're All Insane! Second Edition: Six Reasons Why You're Insane*. FitzMaurice Publishers, Omaha, NE. 1991, 2012. Available for computers, smartphones, tablets, and e-readers from Amazon, Barnes & Noble, Google, Kobo, and Apple.

FitzMaurice, Kevin Everett. *How to Govern Anything: Ocean Government*. FitzMaurice Publishers, Omaha, NE. 2012. Available for computers, smartphones, tablets, and e-readers from Amazon, Barnes & Noble, Google, Kobo, and Apple.

FitzMaurice, Kevin Everett. *3D: Daily Does of Discernment: 2006*. FitzMaurice Publishers, Omaha, NE. 2012. Available for computers, smartphones, tablets, and e-readers from Amazon, Barnes & Noble, Google, Kobo, and Apple.

FitzMaurice, Kevin Everett. *3D: Daily Does of Discernment: 2007*. FitzMaurice Publishers, Omaha, NE. 2012. Available for computers, smartphones, tablets, and e-readers from Amazon, Barnes & Noble, Google, Kobo, and Apple.

FitzMaurice, Kevin Everett. *The Secret of Maturity, Third Edition*. FitzMaurice Publishers, Omaha, NE. 1989, 1990, 2012. Available for computers, smartphones, tablets, and e-readers from Amazon, Barnes & Noble, Google, Kobo, and Apple.

FitzMaurice, Kevin Everett. *Stress for Success, Second Edition*. FitzMaurice Publishers, Omaha, NE. 2013. Available for computers, smartphones, tablets, and e-readers from Amazon, Barnes & Noble, Google, Kobo, and Apple.

FitzMaurice, Kevin Everett. *3D: Daily Does of Discernment: 2008*. FitzMaurice Publishers, Omaha, NE. 2013. Available for computers, smartphones, tablets, and e-readers from Amazon, Barnes & Noble, Google, Kobo, and Apple.

FitzMaurice, Kevin Everett. *Self: Who Am I?* FitzMaurice Publishers, Omaha, NE. 2013. Available for computers, smartphones, tablets, and e-readers from Amazon, Barnes & Noble, Google, Kobo, and Apple.

FitzMaurice, Kevin Everett. *3D: Daily Does of Discernment: 2009*. FitzMaurice Publishers, Omaha, NE. 2013. Available for computers, smartphones, tablets, and e-readers from Amazon, Barnes & Noble, Google, Kobo, and Apple.

FitzMaurice, Kevin Everett. *Games Ego Plays*. FitzMaurice Publishers, Portland, OR. 2014. Available for computers, smartphones, tablets, and e-readers from Amazon.

FitzMaurice, Kevin Everett. *Journal Journey from Ego*. FitzMaurice Publishers, Portland, OR. 2014. Available for computers, smartphones, tablets, and e-readers from Amazon.

FitzMaurice, Kevin Everett. *Ego Playground*. FitzMaurice Publishers, Portland, OR. 2014. Available for computers, smartphones, tablets, and e-readers from Amazon.

FitzMaurice, Kevin Everett. *3D: Daily Does of Discernment: 2010*. FitzMaurice Publishers, Portland, OR. 2015. Available for computers, smartphones, tablets, and e-readers from Amazon.

FitzMaurice, Kevin Everett. *What's Your Story?* FitzMaurice Publishers, Portland, OR. 2015. Available for computers, smartphones, tablets, and e-readers from Amazon.

FitzMaurice, Kevin Everett. *World Within: The Inner Life*. FitzMaurice Publishers, Portland, OR. 2016. Available for computers, smartphones, tablets, and e-readers from Amazon.

FitzMaurice, Kevin Everett. *Planet Earth: Insane Asylum for the Universe, Second Edition*. FitzMaurice Publishers,

Portland, OR. 2000, 2016. Available for computers, smartphones, tablets, and e-readers from Amazon.

FitzMaurice, Kevin Everett. *Games Ego Plays, Revised Version*. FitzMaurice Publishers, Portland, OR. 2014, 2017. Available as a paperback book from Amazon.

FitzMaurice, Kevin Everett. *Secret of Maturity, Fourth Edition*. FitzMaurice Publishers, Portland, OR. 1989, 1990, 2012, 2017. Available for computers, smartphones, tablets, e-readers, and in paperback from Amazon.

Frankl, Victor E. *Man's Search for Meaning: An Introduction to Logotherapy.* Beacon Press, Boston. 1959, 1963.

Fromm, Eric. *The Art of Loving*. Harper and Row, New York. 1956.

Goldberg, Marilee C. *The Art of the Question*. John Wiley & Sons, New York. 1998.

Goleman, Daniel. *Emotional Intelligence*. Bantam Books, New York. 1995.

Gordon, Thomas. *Parent Effectiveness Training: The Proven Program for Raising Responsible Children*. Three Rivers Press, New York. 2000.

Hauck, Paul A. *Overcoming the Rating Game: Beyond Self-Love, Beyond Self-Esteem.* Westminster/John Knox Press, Louisville, KY. 1991.

Hedges, Chris. *When Atheism Becomes Religion: America's New Fundamentalists.* Free Press, New York. 2008.

Hoff, Benjamin. *The Tao of Pooh.* Dutton, New York. 1982.

James, Muriel, and Dorothy Jongeward. *Born to Win: Transactional Analysis with Gestalt Experiments.* Addison-Wesley, Reading, MA. 1971.

Kapleau, Philip. *The Three Pillars of Zen: Teaching, Practice, and Enlightenment.* Beacon Press, Boston. 1967.

Kierkegaard, Søren. *The Sickness unto Death: A Christian Psychological Exposition for Upbuilding and Awakening.* Edited and translated by Howard V. Hong and Edna H. Hong. Princeton University Press, Princeton. 1980.

Kierkegaard, Søren. *Purity of Heart Is to Will One Thing: Spiritual Preparation for the Office of Confession.* Translated by Douglas V. Steere. Harper and Row, New York. 1938.

Kierkegaard, Søren. *Works of Love: Some Christian Reflections in the Form of Discourses.* Translated by

Howard V. Hong and Edna H. Hong. Harper and Row, New York. 1962.

Kierkegaard, Søren. *Training in Christianity and the Edifying Discourses*. Translated by Walter Lowrie. Princeton University Press, Princeton. 1967.

Kierkegaard, Søren. *Attack upon "Christendom."* Translated by Walter Lowrie. Princeton University Press, Princeton. 1944.

Kierkegaard, Søren. *Christian Discourses*. Translated by Alas. Princeton University Press, Princeton. 1971.

Kierkegaard, Søren. *Either/Or: Part I.* Edited and translated by Howard V. Hong and Edna H. Hong. Princeton University Press, Princeton. 1987.

Kohlberg, Lawrence. "Stage and Sequence: The Cognitive-Developmental Approach to Socialization." In D. A. Goslin (ed.), *Handbook of Socialization Theory and Research*. Rand McNally, Chicago. 1969.

Korzybski, Alfred. *Science and Sanity: An Introduction to Non-Aristotelian Systems and General Semantics, Fourth Edition*. The International Non-Aristotelian Library Publishing Company, Lakeville, CT. 1958. Charlotte Schuchardt Read.

Krishnamurti, J. [Jiddu]. *The First and Last Freedom.* With a foreword by Aldous Huxley. Harper and Row Publishers, New York. 1954. Krishnamurti Foundation.

Krishnamurti, J. [Jiddu]. *Think on These Things*. Edited by D. Rajagopal. Harper and Row Publishers, New York. 1964. Krishnamurti Foundation.

Krishnamurti, J. [Jiddu]. *Freedom from the Known.* Edited by Mary Lutyens. Harper and Row Publishers, New York. 1969. Krishnamurti Foundation.

Krishnamurti, J. [Jiddu]. *The Flight of the Eagle*. Harper and Row Publishers, New York. 1972. Krishnamurti Foundation.

Laing, R.D. *Knots*. Penguin, London. 1970.

Loftus, Elizabeth F. and Doyle, James M. *Eyewitness Testimony: Civil and Criminal*. Lexis Law Publishers, New York. 1997.

Maultsby, Jr., Maxie C. *Rational Behavioral Therapy.* Prentice-Hall, Englewood Cliffs, NJ. 1984.

Medved, Diane. *The Case Against Divorce*. Ivy Books, New York. 1993.

Mercer, Michael W., and Maryann V. Troiani. *Spontaneous Optimism: Proven Strategies for Health,*

Prosperity and Happiness. Castlegate, Lake Zurich, IL. 1998.

Merton, Thomas. *The Way of Chung Tzu*. New Directions. New York. 1965.

Mills, David. *Overcoming "Self-esteem": Why Our Compulsive Drive for "Self-esteem" Is Anxiety-Provoking, Socially Inhibiting, and Self-Sabotaging*. Pamphlet available from the Albert Ellis Institute for Rational Emotive Behavior Therapy, 45 East 64th Street, New York, NY. 10021-6593. (212) 535–0822.

Müller, F. Max (translator, 1879). *The Upanishads, Vol. I*. Dover Publications, Mineola, NY. 1962.

Nietzsche, Friedrich Wilhelm. *Beyond Good and Evil: Prelude to a Philosophy of the Future*. Translated by R. J. Hollingdale. Penguin Books, New York. 1973.

Olney, Kathryn. "Can Violent Men Be Treated?" *The Family Therapy Networker,* January/February, pp. 12–13. 1994.

Page, Susan. *How One of You Can Bring the Two of You Together: Breakthrough Strategies to Resolve Your Conflict and Reignite Your Love*. Broadway Books, New York. 1997.

Peele, Stanton. *Love and Addiction*. New American Library, New York. 1975.

Plato. *The Republic of Plato*. (See Part II, Book IV, Chapter XIII). Translated, with introduction and Notes, by Frances MacDonald Cornford. Oxford University, New York. 1941.

Rifkin, Jeremy. *Algeny: A New Word—A New World*. In collaboration with Nicanor Perlas. Penguin Books, New York. 1983.

Rosellini, Gale & Worden, Mark. *Of Course You're Angry*. Hazelden, Center City, Minnesota. 1985.

Rogers, Carl R. *On Becoming a Person: A Therapist's View of Psychotherapy*. Houghton Mifflin, Boston. 1961.

Siegel, Bernie S. *Love, Medicine and Miracles: Lessons Learned about Self-healing from a Surgeon's Experience with Exceptional Patients*. Harper and Row, New York. 1986.

Stone, Douglas, Bruce Patton, and Sheila Heen. *Difficult Conversations: How to Discuss What Matters Most*. Viking Press, New York. 1999.

Szasz, Thomas, S. *The Myth of Mental Illness: Foundations of a Theory of Personal Conduct* (revised ed.). Harper and Row, New York. 1974.

Tavris, Carol. *Anger: The Misunderstood Emotion*. Simon and Schuster, New York, N.Y. 1982.

Tzu, Chuang. *The Sayings of Chuang Chou* [Tzu]. Translated by James R. Ware. The New American Library of World Literature, New York. 1963.

Tzu, Lao. *Tao of Lao Tsze*. Translated by Charles H. Mackintosh. The Theosophical Publishing House, Wheaton, IL. 1926.

Tzu, Lao. *The Way of Life: According to Lao Tzu*. Translated by Witter Bynner. Putnam Publishing, New York. 1944.

Tzu, Sun. *The Art of War.* Translated by Thomas Cleary. Shambhala Publications, Boston. 1988.

Vernon, Ann. *Thinking, Feeling, Behaving: An Emotional Education Curriculum for Children/Grades 1-6, Revised Edition*. 2006.

Walen, Susan R., Raymond DiGiuseppe, and Windy Dryden. *A Practitioner's Guide to Rational-Emotive Therapy, Second Edition*. Oxford University Press, New York. 1992.

Weinberg, Harry L. *Levels of Knowing and Existence: Studies in General Semantics*. Harper and Brothers, Publishers, New York. 1959.

Winn, Marie. *The Plug-In Drug, Revised Edition*. Penguin Books, New York. 1985.

How to Read FitzMaurice's Books

Follow the link below to learn how to read FitzMaurice's books on your tablet, smartphone, computer, or e-reader.

http://www.kevinfitzmaurice.com/book_ereader.htm

FitzMaurice's Books

More book titles and book information can be found on Amazon, Barnes & Noble, Google Play, Kobo, and iTunes.

Book Descriptions

Follow the link below to learn more about FitzMaurice's available books:

http://www.kevinfitzmaurice.com/book_descriptions.htm

99¢ Books

Follow the link below to learn more about FitzMaurice's 99¢ books:

http://www.kevinfitzmaurice.com/book_ninetyninecents.htm

How to Change the World

How To Govern Anything is available for $6.99 from the following link:

Amazon, Barnes & Noble, Google, Kobo, and Apple.

How to Live Maturely

The Secret of Maturity, Third Edition is available for 99¢ from the following link:

Amazon, Barnes & Noble, Google, Kobo, and Apple.

How to Make Stress Work for You

Stress for Success, Second Edition is available for 99¢ from the following link:

Amazon, Barnes & Noble, Google, Kobo, and Apple.

How to Have a Super Attitude

Attitude Is All You Need! Second Edition is available for $2.99 from the following link:

Amazon, Barnes & Noble, Google, Kobo, and Apple.

How to End Ego

Ego is available for $9.99 from the following link:

Amazon, Barnes & Noble, Google, Kobo, and Apple.

How to Live a Positive Life

Not is available for $9.99 from the following link:

Amazon, Barnes & Noble, Google, Kobo, and Apple.

How to Use CBT for Self-Help

Garden is available for $9.99 from the following link:

Amazon, Barnes & Noble, Google, Kobo, and Apple.

How to Practice Instant Yoga

Breathe is available for $9.99 from the following link:

Amazon, Barnes & Noble, Google, Kobo, and Apple.

Enjoy!

Made in United States
North Haven, CT
30 July 2022

22023980R00193